Circular Walks

in

Central Devon

Simone Stanbrook–Byrne

and

James Clancy

CULM VALLEY PUBLISHING

Published by

Culm Valley Publishing Ltd
Culmcott House
Mill Street, Uffculme
Cullompton, Devon
EX15 3AT, UK
Tel: +44(0)1884 849085
Fax: +44(0)1884 840251
E-mail: info@culmvalleypublishing.co.uk
Website: www.culmvalleypublishing.co.uk

While every effort has been made to ensure the accuracy of the information contained in
this book, the publisher and authors accepts no liability for incorrect information
regarding public footpaths and rights of way. Neither Culm Valley Publishing Ltd nor
the authors shall be liable for any damages whatsoever arising in any way from the use of
or inability to use this book, or any material contained within it, or from any action or
decision taken as a result of using this book. Follow the country code.

First published 2011

ISBN 978-1-907942-01-3 paperback

British Library Cataloguing-in-Publication Data
A catalogue record for this book is available from the British Library

Typeset by Culm Valley Publishing Ltd
Printed and bound by T.J. International Ltd, Padstow, Cornwall
Cover image: View from near Christ Cross across the Exe Valley (Silverton Walk)

Contents

Introduction

On any walk common sense must prevail: be properly shod and take care where you put your feet, be prepared for any kind of weather, take food and first aid supplies with you and make sure someone knows where you're going. Mobile phones are often useless in the middle of nowhere.

We also feel it's **imperative** that you take the **correct OS map** with you plus a **compass**, and are conversant with their use. Our sketch maps are precisely that – sketches – and are for rough guidance only and are not to scale. This book mostly uses **OS Explorer 114: Exeter & the Exe Valley** but the Culmstock route requires **OS Explorer 128: Taunton & the Blackdown Hills**.

You know you've had a good day's walking when you get home safely at the end of it.

Follow the countryside code:
www.naturalengland.org.uk/ourwork/enjoying/countrysidecode/def
ault.aspx

Disclaimer

Points that should be borne in mind:

Public footpaths can be legally re-routed from the path shown on the map. In such cases they are usually clearly signposted. Where this has happened before the time of writing it has been noted in the text.

Most public footpaths are on private land. Please respect this.

Don't be surprised to find livestock grazing on public footpaths – and treat all animals with caution and respect.

If a field is planted with crops across a footpath, provision is usually made around the edge of the field.

Landmarks can change: trees and hedges may disappear; streams can dry up in warm weather; stiles turn into gates and vice versa; fences appear where previously there was no boundary. Even views are different as the seasons change. In such cases a modicum of common sense must be exercised – in conjunction with the map.

Public footpaths are at times blocked by barbed wire etc. Should this render the route impassable find the shortest detour around that section.

Please leave gates as you find them and if you have to climb them do so at the hinge end where it's stronger.

Exercise caution on wet stiles – they can be extremely slippery.

Take all your rubbish with you, don't damage anything during the walk and don't pick plants.

Keep your dogs under proper control.

We hope that you enjoy these walks without mishap, but urge you to exercise common sense at all times! Neither the authors nor Culm Valley Publishing Ltd. accepts responsibility for any misadventure which may occur during or arise from these walks and suggested routes.

6

Acknowledgements

Our grateful thanks to:

Brian and Jenny Willan;

Graham Parnell of Silverton Local History Society;

Rev'd Nigel Guthrie, Rector of Crediton Parish Church, and Rosemary Barber, Church Warden of Shobrooke Parish Church;

Sarah Childs of West Backstone Farm;

Vera Stuckey for spreading the word;

Tony, Nic, William and Ella.

Walking at Withleigh

Walk Locations

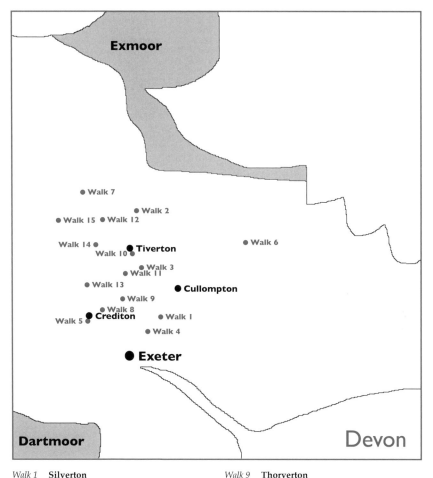

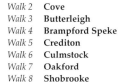

Walk 1	Silverton		*Walk 9*	Thorverton
Walk 2	Cove		*Walk 10*	Tiverton
Walk 3	Butterleigh		*Walk 11*	Bickleigh & Cadeleigh
Walk 4	Brampford Speke		*Walk 12*	Stoodleigh
Walk 5	Crediton		*Walk 13*	Kennerleigh & Woolfardisworthy
Walk 6	Culmstock		*Walk 14*	Withleigh
Walk 7	Oakford		*Walk 15*	Rackenford
Walk 8	Shobrooke			

Silverton

Silverton is a very well-appointed village with a couple of shops and a post office in addition to three pubs. This walk, a favourite with one of the authors who lives just off the route, is generally uphill on the way out but very downhill on the return journey. It affords glorious viewpoints along the way and the chance of seeing roe deer. One short stretch, along the ancient Green Lane, has a spring rising across it, so wellies are the best footwear. Some of the route follows very quiet lanes which make for easy walking.

Map: OS Explorer 114, Exeter & the Exe Valley 1:25 000

Start point: Coach Road, Silverton. Post code EX5 4JY. Grid ref SS959031

Directions to start: Silverton's situation is roughly equidistant between Tiverton and Exeter, just off the A396. It can also be reached by exiting the M5 at junctions 28 & 29

Distance: 4 miles / 6.4km

Parking: On Coach Road near Silverton Primary School or in the free car park on Wyndham Road, signposted from village centre

Facilities: Silverton boasts three well-regarded pubs: The Lamb (01392 860272); The Silverton Inn (01392 860196); The Three Tuns (01392 860352)

Nearby places to stay: The Silverton Inn (01392 860196); The Three Tuns (01392 860352)

Possible birds include: Blackbird, blue tit, buzzard, carrion crow, goldfinch, great spotted woodpecker, green woodpecker, long tailed tit, redwing, robin, rook, skylark, starling

Authors' tip: On the first Saturday morning of every month Silverton holds a local produce market in the community hall and on the first Saturday in August every year it hosts a massive Street Market lasting the entire day with events going on into the evening

---

On Coach Road face the school buildings and you will see a footpath sign to the right of the school, pointing up steps. Take this narrow path with gardens on your right and the school on your left and keep along here as it takes a sharp left turn round the perimeter of the school field. At the end of the path, on the right,

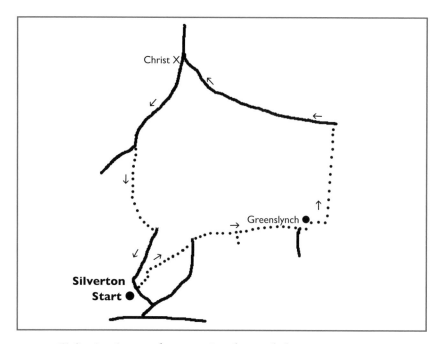

you will find a footpath gate. Go through here and enter a small paddock. Walk straight across, with the fence on your left and buildings to your right, to another footpath gate about 40m away. Beyond here walk ahead along the top of the field with the boundary to your left and the field sloping down to your right. You are now leaving the buildings of Silverton behind you.

Soon you will see a post with a footpath arrow directing you to the right down the field. Follow this to the gate at the bottom and pass through to meet a lane. Turn left for about 50m (note the waterway adjacent to the lane which has the delightful name of Heal-eye Stream), then right at the public footpath which leads off the lane and up a stony track to another footpath gate. Beyond here you will see a yellow-arrowed post, turn left as indicated to follow the left boundary of the field up to yet another footpath gate with three footpath arrows. Pass through here to continue along the narrow, tree-lined path beyond.

Follow this clear path until it emerges by cottages in the tiny hamlet of Greenslynch. The path meets a tarmac drive at a bend. Leave the path to continue in the same direction along the drive, passing Greenslynch Farm on your left and then bending left with the drive until it reaches the entrance gates to Greenslynch Barton. Turn right here, away from the buildings, to head uphill on a stony track.

A few hundred metres further on the broad track swings left. Follow it and keep on this ancient Green Lane for ¾ mile, negotiating the muddy bits, as it climbs up and up to meet a lane. At the lane turn left. The views from this high, airy place are phenomenal. You reach a wide, open section of lane which is a good vantage point. To the left (roughly south) you can see out across the Culm Valley to the Exe Estuary at Dawlish Warren and beyond to ships at sea. Dartmoor is to the south west, to the south east is the Sidmouth Gap and to the north east, when you find a gap in the hedge, you can see across to the Blackdown Hills (Culmstock

View from near Christ Cross across the Exe Valley

"Islands" in the mist

Walk). Look south west again and, closer than Dartmoor and just across the Exe Valley, you will see the lone pine on Raddon Hills, which you meet on the Thorverton Walk. Savour it all.

At Christ Cross (pronounced locally as criss-cross), turn left towards Silverton. At strategic gates there are good views to your right from this lane across the Exe Valley. Eventually you pass the entrance to Roach Farm on your left and then Land Farm on your right, birthplace of Exe Valley Brewery beers, deep joy. Continue downhill and about ¾ mile from Christ Cross the lane bends sharply right. At this point you will see a footpath sign directing you left up to a gate. Follow this sign and beyond the gate a narrow grassy path, with a hedge on the left and a fence on the right, leads you gently downhill towards Silverton. There are lovely views of the village as you approach. This path emerges through a gate onto a tarmac drive. Turn right here to continue downhill, back to the school and Coach Road.

Cromwellian Occupation of Silverton

During the English Civil War this quiet, agricultural area was very much dragged into the fray. In October 1645, Cromwell's soldiers, under the command of Thomas Fairfax, marched on Silverton, probably approaching from Christ Cross down what is now the High Street, before continuing a couple of days later to Newton St. Cyres. Then in 1646 Fairfax and the besieging army were quartered here, taking over many of the local farms and cottages with encampments around the village. During this time around five thousand soldiers, including mercenaries from Europe and possibly Mesopotamia (present day Iraq), swamped the village as they prepared to attack Exeter. Imagine the disruption and suffering this would have caused to hard-pressed familiess and the subsequent privation after feeding this many uninvited guests. Reputedly, thirty cows were slaughtered for one midday meal.

Footpath above Silverton

Towards Killerton across the Culm Valley

Cove

This walk starts at just about its highest point and offers some thirst-quenching views, easy farmland walking and beautiful wooded paths, alive with birdsong. Some very quiet lane-walking is involved. It finishes with a bit of a climb.

Map: OS Explorer 114, Exeter & the Exe Valley 1:25 000	
Start point: Van Post Cross – no post code. Grid ref: SS974190	
Directions to start: Van Post Cross is reached on the old back road between Tiverton and Bampton, about 3 miles north of Chettiscombe	
Distance: 5 miles / 8km	
Parking: There is a handy lay-by on the road at Van Post Cross	
Facilities: None en route, however Bampton boasts the wonderful Quarryman's Rest (01398 331480) which serves excellent food and is worth the short drive to try it out	
Nearby places to stay: Blackberries, Bampton (01398 331842); Quarryman's Rest (01398 331480)	
Possible birds include: Buzzard, carrion crow, chiffchaff, great tit, long tailed tit, nuthatch, pheasant, raven, woodpigeon, wren	
Authors' tip: Just north of Cove the market town of Bampton hosts an annual fair on the last Thursday of October. This traditional event existed even before being granted a royal charter in 1258. It is one of the oldest such fairs in England. Visit Bampton during the summer for its wonderful floral displays. It has won Britain in Bloom on many occasions	

From the crossroads walk along the lane signposted towards Huntsham. You will see the locally well-known weather radar 'golf ball'. At the next crossroads, Cobbacombe Cross, beside a house called Doctorsdown Cottage, turn left towards Bampton. Just under ½ mile from Cobbacombe Cross the lane takes a distinct left bend and a track continues ahead. This is Nine Ash Cross, although evidence of just nine ashes is difficult to see. Take the track, the woodland of Great Brake is to your right. In a little over ½ mile a broad left turn appears. Take it and soon a beautifully-framed view to the hills between Bampton and Shillingford will

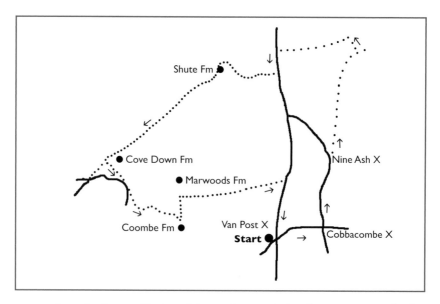

open ahead of you. Enjoy this and turn left when you reach the fence, still following a broad track.

Keep on this track until it reaches the lane. Turn left here as far as the drive of Shute Farm. Here you will see a bridleway sign on the right, go down the drive and at the farm buildings look out for the blue bridleway arrow pointing you right through a gate to avoid walking through their garden. Once through this gate follow the line of the fence on your left to another gate in the boundary ahead. Beyond this to the left you will see yet another gate 30m away. Go through here and walk straight ahead, downhill, with the fence and farmhouse to your left. There are more lovely views ahead.

Continue through another gate and down the next field in the same direction to the bottom corner. You will find a gate ahead of you (ignore the one to the left), beyond which you bear diagonally right to another gate about 30m away with a bridleway arrow. The path drops down into woodland, keep with it, this is a lovely stretch of walking. Look out for a post with a blue arrow at an indistinct fork, which directs you left. The path leads down to a gate in a damp, verdant area of woodland, which can be swimming in birdsong. Go through the gate, across a small stream, ahead for a few metres and then turn left as directed by the blue arrow along a clear path.

At the next gate continue ahead. The path leaves the woodland and you find yourself walking above a valley to the left with a hillside sloping up to your right. You have a really good chance of seeing red deer round here. Continue ahead with the fence on your right. At the end of the field you find another gate with bridleway arrows. Pass through this gate then continue in the same direction but now with the boundary to your left. You will see a ruined building ahead of you. Walk past this building on your left to leave the field in the corner, via a gate. Bear diagonally right beyond this for a few metres to another arrowed gate. Beyond here walk across the bottom of a field with the boundary to your left.

Looking north to the hills between Bampton and Shillingford

In the corner leave through another gate and walk down the bridleway beyond, which passes between fences. You will see a house to your right. At the bottom of the track you meet the drive to Cove Down Farm. Here you will see a direction post. Walk across the drive to pick up the signed footpath which passes through a gate (the bridleway continues sharply right along the drive at this point, but you are now leaving that).

Beyond the gate head down the field to the opposite corner in the direction indicated by the footpath sign. At the bottom you will find a yellow arrow directing you across a footbridge. This leads to a lane on which you turn left, with a stream babbling along beside you on the left. At a gate to Longham Farm continue up their concrete drive and when you reach the buildings walk past the house on your left then beyond it turn left to walk between the house and a barn conversion with a lovely stained glass window. The track goes uphill to bear right and leads between hedges for about 20m to a gate. Go through the next field with the hedge on your right and at the end leave through another gate, pausing to take in the views behind you. This gate leads to a path, hedged on both sides, keep with the path as far as another gate with a yellow

Weather Radar

During the early part of this walk it is impossible not to notice the remarkable sight of a giant golf ball high up in the fields ahead, towards Huntsham. This construction is a weather surveillance radar which monitors rainfall, snow etc. in order to predict where it will fall and its likely intensity. During WWII it was discovered that Radar (Radio Detection and Ranging) worked on raindrops and this was later put to use in weather forecasting. This site is administered by Devon CC, the Met Office and the National Rivers Authority.

Rolling hillsides

arrow. Beyond here you will see more farm buildings. This is Coombe Farm. Keep on the path to pass a tractor shed / log store on your left, the farmhouse will appear down to your right. Beyond the shed you will see a yellow arrowed gate. Go through here and bear left back on yourself following the left hand boundary of the field you have entered as it goes uphill. It's a bit of a trudge up to a small gate leading onto a narrow path. Follow this path and after about 30m you meet the drive to Marwoods Farm. Turn right here away from the farm and follow the drive through fields until you reach the lane. If you need to pause for breath glance behind for dramatic views of old quarries away to the right. When you reach the lane turn right back to Van Post Cross about ½ mile away. Just before you get there you will see a gap in the hedge on your right leading to a 'Cycle Rest', kindly set aside by the landowner, to sustain those on Sustrans Route 3. There's a welcome bench in here overlooking more stunning views. Nice for cyclists. As walkers, technically you haven't earned it!

Walk 3
Butterleigh

Butterleigh is a delightful village and the Burn Valley, through which this walk passes, is renowned for its spring flowers. This is a lovely, mostly level route but can be a bit muddy and the stiles aren't always dog-friendly. We had to lift Pandora over them so if you own a Great Dane you may be in trouble. Horse-lovers will enjoy this walk – there are plenty to see.

Map: OS Explorer 114, Exeter & the Exe Valley 1:25 000

Start point: Butterleigh village. Post code EX15 1PN. Grid ref SS974081

Directions to start: Butterleigh is in the middle of nowhere, signed off the A396 Exeter–Tiverton road. It can also be accessed from the un-numbered back road between Cullompton and Tiverton

Distance: 3 miles / 4.8km

Parking: In the car park by Butterleigh Village Hall, opposite the Inn

Facilities: The Butterleigh Inn: (01884 855407)

Nearby places to stay: The Butterleigh Inn (01884 855407); Lower Ford Farm, Cullompton – but close to Butterleigh (01884 252354); Burrow Farm, Burrow Corner (01884 855292)

Possible birds include: Blackbird, blue tit, bullfinch, buzzard, goldfinch, great spotted woodpecker, great tit, green woodpecker, long tailed tit, robin, woodpigeon. More rarely, red kite have visited the farmland in this area

Authors' tip: Not really a tip, but a notable note: this tiny village has, in recent years, had two Olympic medallists, one for bobsleigh and one for kayaking

Leave the car park and turn left along the lane, downhill through the village. At the T-junction, with Hatswell Cottages ahead of you, turn right towards Tiverton. After about 50m turn left on the well-signed footpath and walk down the field with the boundary on your left, leaving Butterleigh behind you. At the end of the field cross the stile beside the gate and continue straight ahead across the next field for a short distance to a kissing gate with a footpath sign.

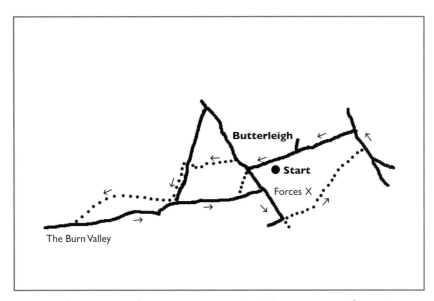

Beyond here cross the lane diagonally left, negotiate the stile and once in the field turn sharp left to follow the hedge on your left, the buildings of Filbrook Farm are down to your right. Follow this boundary on your left as it bears right and leads you to another stile. After this bear slightly right through the next field in the direction of the yellow arrow to a little wooden footbridge.

Cross the bridge and notice the arrow on its far end. Follow its direction. There is a boundary to your right for a few metres and you then pass between trees, continuing in a pretty straight line to cross the drive to Underleigh House. Just after crossing the drive you will meet another stile, about 150m from the footbridge.

Beyond this stile continue ahead as directed by another arrow to yet another stile about 100m away. After this stile bear right up the field towards a house and just before you reach it, in the boundary near the corner, you will find another stile. Cross here and turn left along the drive, passing the house on your left. As the drive swings left go straight ahead across another stile and continue in pretty much the same direction down the next field towards the far boundary and the buildings of Higher Brithayes Farm. The Burn River is down to your left.

When you reach the boundary in front of the farm buildings you will find a stile onto a footbridge followed by another stile on the other side. Cross here and bear left through the next field with rising ground and barns to your right. Skirt this slope keeping the field boundary down to your left and you will find a stile followed by a plank bridge which leads onto the lane.

On the lane turn left. You are now walking through the Burn Valley back towards Butterleigh. Follow this lane, as it passes several farm drives, for some distance until you pass Butterleigh Mill. Just beyond here ignore a left turn and continue on the lane until you reach Forces Cross, back at the edge of the village. Turn right here towards Silverton, away from the tempting sign to the

Footpath above the Burn Valley

One of many ponies en route

Inn. (Unless you wish to shorten the walk, in which case go left here and then next right to return to the car park.)

Follow the lane as it starts to go uphill, passing Butterleigh House and Butterleigh Cottage on your left. As the lane takes a sharp right turn go left on the public bridleway (NOT ahead on the footpath) and follow this attractive bridleway (known locally as Parsonage Lane) until it emerges onto a farm drive. Turn left here and follow this drive until you reach a lane.

Once at the lane glance up to your right at the attractive Hillersdon Wood, cladding the hillside above you, then turn left along the lane and continue as far as the next tiny crossroads. Turn left here and follow the lane back to the centre of the village and your car.

Beating the Bounds

The tradition of Beating the Bounds has, in recent years, been revived as an annual event in Butterleigh. Before the advent of written parish records, boundaries were imprinted on the memory of parishioners by means of a perambulation during which various boundary points were noted. Some sources say that the heads of small boys were beaten against each boundary marker to make them remember but nothing quite this brutal happens nowadays in Butterleigh. Instead, sticks are used against trees and gate posts and each boundary marked 'SMPB' — St. Matthew's Parish Boundary. The parish is so tiny that it takes just a couple of hours to walk its perimeter.

Walk 4
Brampford Speke

This easy to follow walk is set in the verdant plains of the Exe Valley so is level walking – something quite rare in this area. The walk takes in a circular section of the long-distance Exe Valley Way and part of the Devonshire Heartland Way.

Map: OS Explorer 114, Exeter & the Exe Valley 1:25 000

Start point: Chapel Road, Brampford Speke. Post code EX5 5HE. Grid ref SX926984

Directions to start: Brampford Speke is north west of Exeter and can be accessed off the A377 Exeter–Crediton road, or the A396 Exeter–Tiverton road, via Thorverton

Distance: 3½ or 6 miles / 5.6 or 10km

Parking: On-road near Brampford Speke Primary School and Exe Valley Tea Shop

Facilities: The Lazy Toad (01392 841591) serves excellent food and drink and the Exe Valley Tea Shop (01392 841785) is a little gem which doubles up as a village shop. Although not directly on the route there are places in Thorverton for refreshment such as The Thorverton Arms (01392 860205)

Nearby places to stay: Barnhill Cottage, Brampford Speke (01392 841785)

Possible birds include: Blackbird, blue tit, carrion crow, chaffinch, coal tit, goldfinch, great tit, grey heron, house sparrow, jackdaw, kestrel, kingfisher, long tailed tit, magpie, mallard, mute swan, pheasant, robin, rook, sand martin, swallow, swift, woodpigeon

Authors' tip: Do this walk on a Sunday morning and you may be rewarded with the atmospheric sound of church bells wafting over the Exe Valley from all the surrounding villages

At the end of Chapel Road, with the school on your right, you will see a footpath sign directing you down a tarmac path. Descend this, there is a high bank on your left and a handrail on your right. This is the Devonshire Heartland Way which runs concurrent with the Exe Valley Way for some of this walk. Cross the River Exe on the footbridge, passing through the bridge gate and turn left on the clear path. You have a fence to your right and are passing the

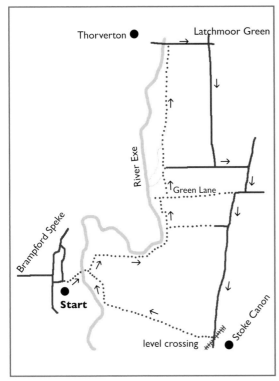

gardens belonging to the old Station House and converted station buildings, now idyllically-situated private houses.

Beyond their gardens you will see a footpath sign directing you right. Take this, go through a kissing gate and then walk straight ahead with the boundary on your right. Continue at the next gate, hedge still on your right, and this line will lead you to a double kissing gate. The River Exe is down to your left and the village you can see over to the right, with its prominent church tower, is Stoke Canon.

Follow the well-trodden path through the field beside the river. At the end of this field cross the stile to continue with the river on your left until it takes a very sweeping left bend. Follow it round to the end of the field then bear slightly right to leave the field on a track through a gap in the hedge, the river now meandering off without you.

The track leads to another kissing gate. Apply lip balm and pass through to join another track along which you turn left. Follow this track when it eventually bends sharp left, followed after a short distance by a sharp right. At the **second sharp right turn** (at which

Route of the old Exe Valley Line

you ignore a smaller path left) you are joining a Green Lane. Those following the shorter route should keep ahead on this Green Lane to rejoin the longer route at (*) below.

Those on the longer route turn left off the Green Lane after about 100m. Soon you will see the Netherexe Church of St. John the Baptist in the fields to your left. This delightful little church, dating back to the 15th C., is still in use, and manages very well without water, gas or electricity, relying on candles and goodwill for light and warmth. When you reach the T-junction turn left on the track (you can also access a path here across the field to visit the church if you wish). You will almost immediately see a footpath and Exe Valley Way sign directing you right into a field. Take this and walk through the field in the direction indicated.

Cross the stile at the end of the field. You will find a small stretch of water on your left. Follow this to its end, bear left through a gap and then continue in the same direction as before, now with the boundary on your right. A yellow arrow helps direct you. Soon you will see another small body of water under the trees on your right. Beyond here keep on in the same direction through open farmland, footpath arrows will reassure you that you're on the right line, which is pretty unvarying until you reach the river again. Turn right along it, keeping the water to your left. In the corner of the field go through the kissing gate and then continue to walk with the river on your left as before. It was along here that

Across the River Exe towards Brampford Speke

we saw a kingfisher. The buildings and cricket pitch of Thorverton come into view and soon you pass Thorverton Weir on your left. Ascend steps at the end of the field, beside the weir workings, and emerge onto the road. Those wishing to visit Thorverton can turn left here into the village.

Otherwise, turn right along the road until you reach the houses of Latchmoor Green about ¼ mile away. At the crossroads turn right between the two white cottages, along the lane signposted to Netherexe. Although you are now walking on lanes they are extremely quiet, more like tarmac footpaths. After about 1 mile you reach a T-junction with two attractive red brick houses on the right. Turn left – you will see an Exe Valley Way sign here.

Reach another T-junction and turn right towards Rewe. A little further on at the next T-junction the field on the left boasts ancient tumuli, although there isn't much evidence to the naked eye. Turn right here and pass three houses, the last of which is called Burrow Corner, at which point you meet the other end of the Green Lane and those on the shorter route.

(*) The long and short route merge here. Those on the short route turn right, those on the long route turn left, and everyone walks away from the red brick bungalow of Burrow Corner. Pass an ancient stone cross on the right near Burrow Farm and keep ahead on the lane in the same direction. The buildings of Stoke Canon begin to appear ahead of you.

Eventually you pass the barns of Oakhay Barton on your right and beyond the farm you reach a level crossing on your left. If you wish to visit Stoke Canon cross here to walk into the village. Otherwise stay on this side of the railway (this is the West Country to Paddington line) and you will see a clearly marked footpath heading right through a kissing gate. This is a narrow path between fences which leads to another kissing gate and into a field. Keep ahead in the same direction, the fence on your left and Brampford Speke church tower beckoning you from over the trees.

Go through another kissing gate and keep on the clear path which is an old, now dismantled, railway line. This leads between fences

The Exe Valley Line

A section of this walk takes you along the route of what was the Exe Valley Branch Line, part of the Great Western Railway. Now grassy paths and tracks through fields, this line, which opened fully in 1885 and ran from Exeter to Dulverton on the edge of Exmoor, was once alive with steam trains and travellers. Brampford Speke Station closed, along with the entire Exe Valley Line, in 1963, a victim of Beeching's 'reshaping'. The original stationmaster's house and the converted station buildings are now privately owned residences.

to another gate and into a field. Continue along the 'track' and the river comes into view again. Another gate leaves the field and enters an enclosed path. At the next gate you enter a field, leaving the old railway line. Keep ahead at the fork with the boundary on your right. This leads to a wooden footbridge. Cross here and continue with the fence on your right to walk across the field to the footbridge across the Exe and the path back up into Brampford Speke.

Approaching Brampford Speke along the disused railway

Crediton

This short walk is a little gem, with glorious views, a pretty hamlet, tranquil river valley and ancient rights of way.

Map: OS Explorer 114, Exeter & the Exe Valley 1:25 000

Start point: The top of Barnfield, Crediton (adjacent to the buildings of Queen Elizabeth Community College). Post code EX17 3HX. Grid ref SS831001

Directions to start: Crediton is on the A377 north west of Exeter

Distance: 2½ miles / 4km

Parking: Park on-road near the school

Facilities: Crediton has lots of places to eat if you explore the town centre, but if you prefer a country pub just outside the town The Lamb (01363 773676) in Sandford, which is 2 miles away, comes very highly recommended

Nearby places to stay: Warren's Farm, Yeoford (01363 84304)

Possible birds include: Blue tit, carrion crow, chaffinch, goldfinch, little egret, raven, woodpigeon

Authors' tip: If you fancy exploring by train rather than walking, Crediton is on the Exeter–Barnstaple line – a very picturesque stretch of railway known as The Tarka Line. One of the authors used to live in this area, at which time those wishing to catch this train at Yeoford had to flag it down

---

Walk up Barnfield, the school is on your right and continue past the school along the clear track at the end of the road. The track leads past Yeoland House, and just beyond the house on the left is a kissing gate. Go through here and follow the arrow which points you diagonally right across the field to another gate. Beyond here you continue along the same line to another gate across the field. Once through here turn left and follow the line of the hedge on your left for about 100m to yet another gate which you can see ahead. There is a good panorama to your right here towards Dartmoor which is visible on a clear day. Through the next gate and head down through the field beyond in the same line as before – keep the hedge on your left and ignore the path which is pointed to the right.

Looking south west from the footpath between Crediton and Salmonhutch

You begin to descend now and take in more wonderful views. Very soon the hamlet of Salmonhutch comes into sight below you with its level crossing (the crossing, curiously, is called Salmon Pool). Head down the field and at the bottom right hand corner leave through the kissing gate onto the lane. Turn left and cross the level crossing – this is the picturesque train line between Exeter and Barnstaple – The Tarka Line. Continue past the terrace of cottages on your left. A few metres further along the lane you will see a public footpath sign on the left, crossing a stile. Take this. The path follows the line of the garden fence on your left to a gate at the end of the field, but some people follow the right hand hedge down to the delightfully meandering River Yeo to walk beside the water, although this is not a public right of way. Leave through the kissing gate, you will see the yellow arrow to direct you, and after another 50m pass through another gate. Keep straight ahead through the next field with the hedge on your left and the river away to the right.

Level crossing at Salmonhutch

At the end of this next field the river once again meanders in to meet the path. Go through the gate, cross the little footbridge over a tributary stream and follow the path with the fence on your left and the river down on the right. The next kissing gate continues onto a broader path in the same direction. You are now walking through a field which widens as the river strolls off to the right. Keep alongside the hedge on your left and near the end of the field leave via the kissing gate beneath a rather splendid old oak.

Turn left along the track, pass round the metal gate and continue to the railway line. The footpath goes through a gate, across the railway to another gate (exercise caution) and emerges onto a lane. Turn left along this lane which forks after about 100m. Take the right hand fork which will lead you to a red brick farmhouse, Lower Parks Farm. Walk round the right hand end of the house and continue along the track with the buildings on your left.

Keep on this track as it heads up between hedges to leave the farm buildings behind – through a gate on your right you will soon see the school buildings ahead of you on the skyline. This feels like a very ancient right of way – one which you can imagine has seen centuries of passers-by. About 0.3 of a mile from the farm the track broadens out at a meeting of gates. At this point bear right and then quickly right again, across a stile, along another distinct track. After wet weather this can be a little boggy. The track eventually

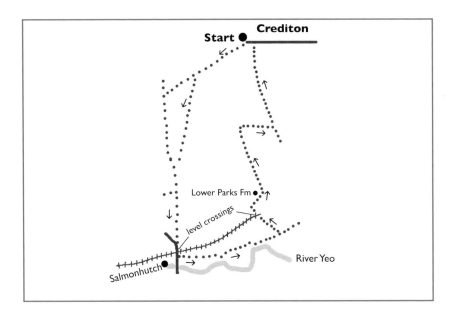

Yeoton Bridge spanning the River Yeo

Crediton

St. Boniface, the Patron Saint of Germany, was born in Crediton circa 680. He was martyred in 754. In Saxon times permission was granted for the foundation of a monastery here. Due to ecclesiastical reorganisation in the early 10th C. Crediton's church subsequently assumed the status of a cathedral. This was probably wooden in construction, like other Saxon cathedrals, and is thought to have occupied a site to the north of the current church. In 909 Edwulf became the first Bishop of Crediton and then in 1050 the bishop's see and the cathedral were moved to Exeter. In 1897 Crediton was appointed a suffragan bishopric as part of the Exeter Diocese and this continues to the present day. Much of Crediton's wealth during the 16th C. derived from the wool trade when Crediton cloth was exported all over the known world.

emerges at a tarmac crossing path adjacent to gardens. Turn left – on your left now is a playing field and playground and ahead is a kissing gate. Go through here and continue – there is a field to your left and houses to the right. This final stretch of the walk has lovely views towards Dartmoor to the left. Keep ahead with the fence on your left and at the end of the field go through a kissing gate onto a path which leads behind the gardens of houses. This emerges back at the top of Barnfield.

Walk 6
Culmstock & Culm Davy

This is a lovely route with some of the most stunning views that inland Devon has to offer. There are some ascents, but nothing too onerous. Some stretches can be muddy.

Map: OS Explorer 128, Taunton & the Blackdown Hills 1:25 000

Start point: Culmstock Village – War Memorial on The Cleave. Post code EX15 3JH. Grid ref ST101136

Directions to start: Culmstock is north east of Cullompton and can be accessed off the A38 on the B3391

Distance: 6¾ miles / 10.9km

Parking: Park in the centre of the village – there is plenty of on-road parking

Facilities: Although this walk doesn't pass any watering holes or toilets outside the village, Culmstock itself has two very good places for refreshment. The Strand Stores (01884 840232) is an excellent village shop and delicatessen with a wonderful café. We highly recommend this, along with the Culm Valley Inn (01884 840354) which is renowned for its good food and ales

Nearby places to stay: The Strand Stores (01884 840232)

Possible birds include: Blue tit, buzzard, carrion crow, chiffchaff, collared dove, dunnock, goldfinch, green woodpecker, grey wagtail, house martin, house sparrow, jay, kestrel, magpie, nuthatch, stonechat, swallow, woodpigeon

Authors' tip: For those preferring a riverside walk rather than the circular route, a stroll along the banks of the River Culm to Hunkin Wood, and beyond that to Uffculme, is an easy and bird-rich amble. Little egret, kingfisher, dipper, grey heron, sand martin, and tree creepers are regularly seen, amongst many others. Goosanders are a rarer treat. This path is accessed beside the bridge, across the road from the Culm Valley Inn

---

Leave the War Memorial, passing The Strand Stores on your left. The River Culm is on your right. Cross the ancient stone bridge and continue on the road past the Culm Valley Inn. At the school the road forks. Wellington and Tiverton are signposted to the left but you keep ahead here, walking up Hunters Hill. You will also see the Village Hall signposted to your right.

The houses gradually drop away behind you and the lane bends left signposted Woodgate ½, Beacon 1. Go right here, which isn't

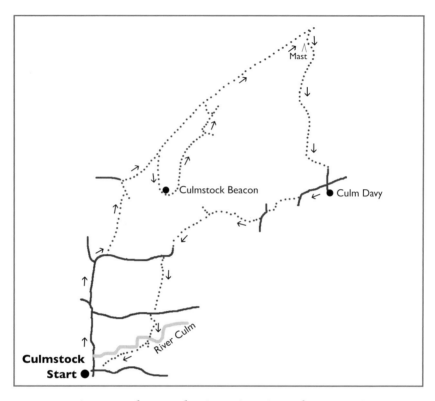

signposted to anything. The lane bends right and after about 200m take the footpath directing you left off this lane along a farm track. Another 200m along the track you find a stile on your right. Cross here into the field, glancing back as you do to see the distant spire of St. Mary's Church in Uffculme. As you cross this farmland you will periodically see yellow footpath arrows to help guide you.

Bear diagonally left across the field towards farm buildings. You will see another stile by which to leave the field. At the next stile glance back to where you can see Culmstock Church. Once over this stile, pass through the gate opposite and go straight ahead, passing farm buildings on your left. Continue up the left hand boundary of the field you are in (this may require circumnavigating a store of silage first!). Towards the top, the hedge on the left gives way to an old stone wall. At the top corner of the field pass through a gate onto a track.

Follow this, it may be damp underfoot, until you meet a three-way finger post. Turn left here, soon passing a house on your left. The track becomes tarmac and at the T-junction, where you will see more houses ahead of you, turn right uphill on a broad track. After about 100m pass through a gate and continue up the track.

When you meet a broad track on your right (this is just after a narrower track to the right) take this and follow it as it wends its panoramic way to Culmstock Beacon. This is an amazing place, both for the thirst-quenching views and the history. The beacon hut probably dates from the 16thC although some sources give it as possibly medieval (see tinted box feature, page 41). Here you will also find a trig point and a beautifully-constructed bench,

The view from Culmstock Beacon

Across the Culm Valley

created by the children of Culmstock Primary School, situated in the valley below you and which you passed earlier.

A few metres east of the beacon is a wide, grassy area from which three distinct paths head off in different directions. With the beacon hut behind you and the paths ahead of you, you need the right hand path, heading roughly east, with the edge of the beacon hill to your right. Jaw-dropping views open up to your right over the Culm Valley. Keep on this path as it enters trees and bends left. Continue with the fence on your right, beyond which are more wonderful views, ignoring any paths off to the left.

Eventually, the open views to your right disappear and are replaced by woodland. You will then soon notice a path off to the left opposite a gate on your right – ignore this gate and continue another 20m or so to another gate. Go through just for a moment to admire the cathedral-like trees. This is Forestry Commission land and the area is particularly beautiful in spring when the young beech leaves give a glorious light effect.

Return back through the gate and from it walk straight ahead on a narrow path which leads to a broad crossing path. Turn right along this grassy track, you are very likely to see ponies grazing around here. Soon there is a fork in the path, bear left on another broad, grassy track. A very big view opens up as this path bears right; below to your left there is a vast expanse of countryside with a comparatively diminutive M5 away down in the valley. This lovely path leads directly to a pond, but on the way you will notice a telecommunications mast to your right. Make a mental note as you will need this landmark later.

When you reach the pond, which will be directly in front of you and is affectionately known by some local schoolchildren as The Pond of Doom, bear right and walk away from it on another grassy track – you can still see the mast. In about 200m you will see another path on the left, take this. It enters trees with a gate ahead into woodland. Go through this gate and walk ahead on the bridleway. Soon you will reach the mast's enclosure on your right. Walk past it and turn immediately right, following the line of its fence on your right along another track. Pass through the gate and head down the track beyond. Eventually, the track bears slightly right, keep on it, ignoring another broad path to your left which comes in to run parallel with your path for a short distance. Continue until the track passes through a gap in an ancient boundary, pass through, you will see a gate on your right but you turn left down another broad track through conifers. Continue as it bends left between a boundary of beech hedging before re-entering conifers. Stay on this track ignoring any side turns until it is joined by another track coming down from the right.

Continue ahead until you emerge from the woods, passing a house on your left. Keep ahead past the house to join a lane, bearing right downhill. This meets another lane at a T-junction with a post box on the left. Go right here and immediately right again, passing the entrance to Chapel Cottage on your left. You are still going downhill on the lane and within 200m you pass a house and barn conversion on your left, followed by another cottage, Canters, on your right.

Continue with the lane as it bends left past the entrance to Culm Davy Farm. Soon you find a public footpath sign on your right, take this. Keep on the track – it takes you to a T-junction with a lane – at which point turn left (there is a sign here saying 'to public footpath' which is the direction you need). Soon you see another public footpath signposted right. Take this.

This track takes you through a gate as it leads you to Pithayne Farm – once more you have lovely views over the Culm Valley and Culmstock to your left. The track runs straight into the farmyard and you will see yellow footpath arrows on a barn wall. Ignore the one pointing right and keep ahead, passing the barns on your left, the farmhouse is ahead and to the right. Just in front of the next set of barns turn left, away from the house to pass through a gate with another yellow arrow. Go through the gate and bear right through the field in the direction of the arrow, now heading for a telegraph pole on which you will see another arrow. Beyond here you will see a gate onto a footbridge. Cross this into the next field and bear diagonally left through this field to a gate down in the far corner.

Go through here and walk straight down the next field with the hedge on your right. At the bottom of the field go right through a gate along a usually-muddy track. Join the lane and continue in the same direction past Pitt Farm. Just beyond the farm buildings look out for a concealed footpath sign pointing you left off the lane through a gate. Follow the track as it leads into the field with the barns on your left. There is a bungalow to your right. Once in the field head straight across to the opposite hedge (there used to be a field boundary here which is still shown on old OS maps, but now you are walking through an open field). When you reach the hedge you will find a tall post with a yellow footpath marker and a stile, these are tucked just behind the corner of the hedge so look out for them. Cross here and bear diagonally left through the next field to the opposite hedge. In the far corner of the field emerge onto the lane through a gate and turn right.

Pass Blackwater Cottage on your left and just beyond here is another footpath sign. Take this, cross the footbridge and thence to a kissing gate into a field. Turn left and you will see another gate a short distance away. Go through here and head across the field beyond to the bridge which you can see spanning the River Culm. Cross the bridge and bear right across the field to another gate. Go

Culmstock Beacon Hut
Situated on the very edge of the Blackdown Hills, high above the village of Culmstock, you will find a monument to a communications system which predates emails and mobile phones by several centuries. This beautifully-constructed, Grade II listed stone hut housed a pole which, protruding through the roof,  supported a beacon fire. This was one of a series of such beacons used to alert the able-bodied men of England to the imminence of attack from the Spanish Armada in the Channel. The hut's windows face in the direction of the two nearest beacons in the chain so that the beacon-keeper could watch for a neighbour's signal whilst sheltering in the hut. There is some debate about the age of the existing hut. It may well date from the late 16thC with later restoration having been carried out, but it is likely that there has been a beacon on the site since medieval times. The word 'beacon' possibly derives from the Saxon word 'becnen'. Devon had more beacons than any other county in England, probably due to its extensive coastline.

through here – sparing a glance back up to Culmstock Beacon. Continue through the next field keeping the river to your right.

At the far end of the field, don't cross the footbridge but leave the field through a kissing gate. Ascend some steps and turn right towards the church tower which you can see nestling ahead of you. Go through another kissing gate and onto a narrow path between some very pretty cottages. This path joins the lane, keep straight ahead passing the church on your left and you will find yourself back in the centre of Culmstock.

River Culm, approaching Culmstock (the Beacon in the background)

Oakford

This walk is a really enjoyable amble, easy to follow and with no very serious inclines or muddy bits. Much of the walk is accompanied by the music of small streams.

Map: OS Explorer 114, Exeter & the Exe Valley 1:25 000	
Start point: Oakford Village. Post code EX16 9ES. Grid ref SS912213	
Directions to start: Oakford is west of Bampton and is signposted off the A396 Tiverton–Dulverton road	
Distance: 4½ miles / 7.2km	
Parking: Park on-road in the village	
Facilities: The Red Lion Inn (01398 351219) in the centre of the village is a pleasant, unspoiled pub which serves hearty food, good ale and conviviality	
Nearby places to stay: The Red Lion Inn (01398 351219); The Bark House, Oakfordbridge (01398 351236)	
Possible birds include: Buzzard, carrion crow, grey heron, raven, swallow, woodpigeon	

Walk up through the village passing the War Memorial on your right and the path to the church on your left. You will see a black and gold fingerpost here. Continue up the road to pass the inn on your right and gradually the buildings of the village drop away behind you. Ignore any footpaths until you are clear of the village.

Just before you reach the brow of the hill, ¼ mile from the centre of the village, you will find farm gates on both sides of the lane and a footpath leading through a kissing gate by the one on the left. Go through here, notice the nice view back down to the church, and head across the field in the direction of the footpath arrow, towards the opposite boundary. This brings you to a gate in the hedge. Pass through and turn right to follow the line of the hedge.

At the end of this field go through a gate into another field, still keeping the boundary on your right. At the end of this second field

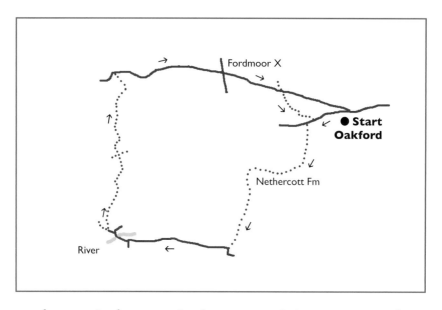

another gate in the corner leads onto a track. You are approaching Nethercott Farm. Turn right on the track which soon leads to the tarmac drive to the farm. Go ahead on this drive for about 10m and you will see a footpath leading right over a stile. Cross this, followed by another stile a few metres beyond. (This is a well-routed, official diversion from the original footpath.) After the second stile turn left to follow the fence with the farm down to your left, heading for the next stile which you can see ahead. When you reach this you will see that it is a double stile, cross here and bear slightly left through the next small field to a gate. Through this, then follow the track to walk away from Nethercott Farm. As the track bends left at the end of the barns leave it and walk ahead across the grass for a few metres, bearing left towards a gate into a field.

Beyond here continue down the next field, bearing slightly right to a gate with a footpath arrow. Go through here and continue on the same line down to the valley bottom. You will soon be walking on a broad and attractive path between gorse – there is a stream in the valley to your right and a conifer plantation cladding the

St Peter's Church

hillside beyond. Listen out for the cronk of ravens. Head for the bottom right hand corner of the field where you will find footbridges crossing the Iron Mill Stream and marshy bits. Beyond the bridges a trodden path leads through a small field, towards a barn, beside which the path exits the field through a gate. Turn right along the lane, passing a stone farmhouse on your right.

Continue on the lane passing Aldridge Mill Cottage and Bellbrook Valley Trout Fishery. Ignore any turnings left or right until, just under ½ mile from Bellbrook, the lane bends round in a sweeping 'U' to cross the busy confluence of rivers. Go round the bend and just before you walk up the other side of the 'U' go left on a 'no through road'.

This lane bends right, passing Spurway Mill Cottage with its bright red letter box on the left. The lane becomes a track and about 50m from the cottage it goes left, at which point a footpath is signed right off the track. Take this and walk ahead through the trees.

The path leads you to a beautifully-situated cottage in the woods. Follow the path behind the cottage and continue in the direction of a yellow footpath arrow, on the track up through the trees. This is a very clear route, slightly uphill through predominantly oak woodland with Combe Water down to your right.

At the time of writing there is a pheasant rearing pen to the left as you progress along this track. As the path goes up into a little pine

South easterly view across Nethercott Wood

wood, about ½ mile from Spurway Mill Cottage, keep straight ahead in the direction of the yellow arrow on the now narrow path. Within 200m of entering the pine trees keep a sharp lookout for an indistinct left hand fork which leads up a slope to a gate into a field. The gate can be seen through the trees if you keep your eyes peeled for it. Pass through this gate and turn right, bearing diagonally right across the field to some lovely oak trees about 150m away. Beneath them you will see another arrow pointing through their boundary. Continue as it directs, diagonally left towards the boundary of the field beyond, where, about 50m beyond the oaks, you will find a rickety and well-concealed footbridge followed by a slope up to a gate. (In the height of summer this can take some finding, it is there!)

Continue through the next field with the hedge on your right. Roughly 70m along this hedge you will find a gap with a yellow waymarker. Pass through here and bear left towards a cottage,

Combe Barton, which you can see beyond the next boundary. The path leads to a gate into their garden through which you have to pass. Bear right across their lawn to pass round the end of the building with the cottage on your left, then leave along the clear track. Please respect their privacy and don't linger, although it is a beautiful place.

The track leads you through Combe Bottom and finally emerges on a lane about 0.3 mile from Combe Barton, at which point you turn right. Keep on here as far as Fordmoor Cross. Continue ahead, signposted for Oakford, and after another 0.3 mile, there is a footpath left which you ignore and very quickly another on the right which you need. The gate is set back right off the lane but there is a yellow arrow to reassure you. Go through here and walk straight ahead at 90° to the lane. You meet a boundary hedge, keep this on your left.

At the bottom of the field go through a kissing gate, down some steps and walk past a pond on your left, the spring-time haunt of some of the most rackety frogs we've ever heard. It can be a bit damp underfoot around here. The narrow path follows the line of the fence on your right, with buildings over to the left. James liked this bit! The fence and footpath take a sharp left round the garden, go with it to reach a kissing gate and pass through. Head down the next field with the boundary on your left. At the bottom there is another kissing gate followed by a couple of footbridges and yet another kissing gate.

Iron Mill Stream
This rather romantically-named waterway is a tributary of the River Exe and was apparently once known as the River Woodburn. It serves as a parish boundary between Oakford and Stoodleigh. Its name is rather curious as documentary evidence of iron smelting in the area is lacking.

From here head up through a small field to a stile. Cross this and head through the next field towards the church tower. At the top right corner of this field leave through a gate and turn left along the lane back to Oakford, its inn and its beautifully light and airy church. Both are worth a visit.

The final stretch back to Oakford

Walk 8
Shobrooke

This is a nice, easy amble. The central section is on quiet lanes which are largely untroubled by traffic and which enjoy some fabulous views.

Map: OS Explorer 114, Exeter & the Exe Valley 1:25 000	
Start point: Shobrooke Village. Post code EX17 1AT. Grid ref SS866013	
Directions to start: Shobrooke is north east of Crediton and can be accessed off the A3072, Crediton–Bickleigh road	
Distance: 2½ or 4 miles / 4 or 6½ km	
Parking: Park on-road in the centre of the village	
Facilities: The Red Lion Inn (01363 772340) is very handy for this walk but if you visit at a time when they are not serving food The Lamb Inn (01363 773676) in Sandford, which is less than 4 miles away, comes very highly recommended	
Nearby places to stay: The Beeches, Shobrooke (01363 775721); The Red Lion Inn (01363 772340); The Lamb Inn, Sandford (01363 773676)	
Possible birds include: Collared dove, heron, house sparrow, linnet, long tailed tit, wheatear, woodpigeon	
Authors' tip: The A3072, from which you may approach Shobrooke, is one of the highest roads in the county. Whilst driving along towards Bickleigh your passengers can experience some spectacular ear-popping scenery	

Walk up out of the village passing the Red Lion on your right. About 200m from the pub, turn left up the steps on a clearly-signed footpath. At the top enter the field and walk diagonally right on the well-trodden path. You can see the church tower peering over the hill in front of you. Head down the slope to a stile near an oak tree – the church and farm buildings are off to the left now and a Dutch barn is in front of you. Leave the field and turn right along the lane for just a few metres to see the little Holy Well with its beautiful wrought iron grille set into the bank on your right (see feature on page 53). St Swithun's Church, which is an easy walk back along the lane, is also worth a visit.

Return to the stile and re-enter the field, this time keeping to the bottom boundary which you follow, the hedge on your right. The

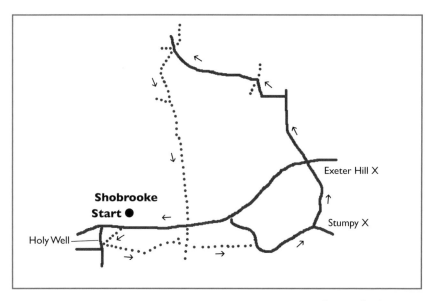

boundary ends at a gap under an oak tree, pass through the gap into the next field and continue in the same direction but now with the hedge on your left. Follow this boundary down the field to where it bends right and soon passes an area of orchard and vegetable garden on the left. Ignore the first footpath on the left and a few metres further on to the right you reach a gate on the left by a telegraph pole. Go through here and directly opposite across a small field you will see a footbridge. Head for this, keeping an eye open for herons, and cross the stream.

Walk straight ahead across the next field, up the gentle slope and through the gate onto the clear footpath which now continues between fences. Pennicot Farm appears ahead of you. At the end of this field cross the stile and turn right along the lane. Follow this windy lane all the way to a T-junction at which you turn left. This junction has the delightful name of Stumpy Cross although there is nothing here to tell you that – a missed opportunity.

Follow this lane as it slopes uphill and at the top pause by the gate in the hedge on your right from which you can look across to

Raddon Hills and the lone pine – a feature of the Thorverton walk. Scanning round to the right from here you can also see across to the Sidmouth Gap.

Continue along the lane and at Exeter Hill Cross go straight ahead, unless you are opting for the shorter route, in which case turn left down the lane and back to Shobrooke.

Those continuing on the longer route can enjoy this narrow, elevated and view-rich lane. Soon you start to descend. About 0.3 mile from the crossroads the lane bends left, keep with it, ignoring the drive ahead to Coombe Barton Farm. At the next bend follow the lane right, ignoring the smaller track directly ahead of you. Soon the lane bends left at which point footpaths lead off left and right. Ignore both of these and continue on the lane for another 0.3 mile.

After passing Lower Coombe Cottages on your left, the lane crosses a stream. Take the footpath a few metres further on your

View from the footpath approaching Shobrooke

Old school bell

The Holy Well

The well was restored by Rev'd Worthington-Jukes, former Rector of Shobrooke, after it had been re-discovered by his dog! It is thought that it was originally a baptismal well and steps inside lead down to the water, the level of which varies considerably depending on rainfall. The lovely wrought iron grille is a very recent addition but the well itself is much older than nearby St. Swithun's church.

left. Here cross the stile off the lane and bear left across the middle of the field heading for a telegraph pole. On this you will see a yellow arrow. Follow this direction to another footpath post which can be seen in the gap in the hedge. Pass through the gap and keep on in the same direction to a couple of plank bridges and stiles in the opposite field boundary.

Beyond here walk through the next field with the boundary on your right. There are some lovely old oaks along here. Cross the stile in the corner and head for the hedge opposite where you will find footpath arrows. Turn left and walk with the hedge on your right as far as the field corner. Here, pass through the gate and beyond join the broad track to continue in the same direction as before, as indicated by the yellow way marker. You are walking through quite an expansive field at this point. When you reach the end of the field keep straight ahead on the track as it leads past Moor Farm. Pass between barns and soon the track leaves the farm behind to reach Shobrooke at a cluster of cottages known as Little Silver. Turn right at the road and you are back on the main street of the village. As you walk through notice the old school bell set in the wall of School Close with a list of the then school governors. There is no longer a school in the village.

Thorverton

This walk will take you up into some of the most stunning views you'll find in this area. The outward journey requires some ascent, but it's very much worth the effort and it's downhill nearly all the way back.

Map: OS Explorer 114, Exeter & the Exe Valley 1:25 000	
Start point: Thorverton Village Car Park. Post code EX5 5NG. Grid ref SS923021	
Directions to start: Thorverton is clearly signposted off the A396 Exeter–Tiverton road. Turn left at The Ruffwell Inn	
Distance: 6 miles / 10km	
Parking: The free car park is clearly signed just off the village centre	
Facilities: The Thorverton Arms (01392 860205); The Ruffwell, Thorverton (01392 860377) which is on the A396 rather than in the village centre	
Nearby places to stay: The Thorverton Arms (01392 860205)	
Possible birds include: Blackbird, blue tit, buzzard, carrion crow, chaffinch, dunnock, great tit, magpie, raven, robin, skylark, wren	
Authors' tip: As you approach Thorverton from the A396 visit the Exe Valley Farm Shop. It's excellent!	

Leave the car park and turn right on the lane heading uphill out of the village. The lane levels out and ahead of you up on the hillside you can see a lone pine, which you will meet later. Continue on the lane passing, on your right, the red brick house of Lynch Farm, with its striking monkey puzzle tree. Three quarters of a mile from the car park you reach Chapel Corner. Continue ahead here towards Shobrooke and Crediton and after another 150m you will see a kissing gate on your right, just past farm buildings and opposite a modern house. Go through here and bear slightly left through the field to follow the boundary on your left. This leads to another kissing gate, go through and continue ahead with the fence to your left and a copse to your right. The path bears slightly right to pass through the end of the copse and leads you to another gate.

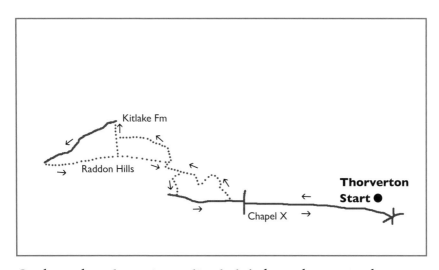

Go through and turn immediately left through a gate to hop over a small stream and then immediately right to walk up through this field with the boundary on your right. Follow this boundary up the field, turning left with it to walk along the top of the field until you find a rickety stile. Cross here (exercise caution, although it may have been renewed by the time you get there) and turn left, keeping the hedge on your left. Follow the hedge round as it skirts the field, until, in the top left corner, you find a plank bridge followed by steps up to a stile. Cross here into the next field and bear diagonally up it in the direction of the yellow arrow on the stile. You will see a waymarker post part way across the field to help guide you. In the top corner, diagonally opposite the point at which you entered, you will find a stile to lead you out of the field. Glance behind you here towards the south east. There are vast views and the Sidmouth Gap is clearly noticeable in the distance.

After the stile you meet a track. Walk straight ahead down to a gate about 30m away with a stile beside it. Cross here and turn right along the tarmac drive, to pass the wonderfully located house of Raddon Hill Lodge on your right with its stunning views. The public footpath goes straight past their garden, respect their

Towards the Iron Age hillfort of Cadbury Castle

privacy please. Keep ahead on the track past the house and very soon you reach the buildings of Raddon Hill Farm at which point the track turns sharply right. Go with it, ignoring a footpath up some steps to your left and continuing a short distance further along the track to a gate on the left with yellow arrows.

Pass through here and head straight up the next field with the boundary on your right – away to your left from here you can see the top section of the lone pine. The field levels out towards the top and ahead of you slightly to the left you will see another yellow-arrowed gate leading left onto a narrow path. Before passing through the gate to join this path enjoy views to the north east and the early Iron Age hillfort of Cadbury Castle.

Once you've looked your fill, join the path which is narrow and wends its way between hedges. From time to time you will find gates to negotiate but the yellow arrows direct you straight on, don't be tempted to veer up left into the fields. Eventually you see the buildings of Kitlake Farm down to your right. When you are almost level with Kitlake you meet another gate and the yellow arrow now directs you left to a small gate through which you leave this narrow path – don't be tempted to leave it any earlier than this.

Go left off the path, through the gate and then immediately right to follow the field boundary on your right. After about 50m you reach another yellow-arrowed gate. Pass through and continue ahead with the boundary on your right until you reach the end of the next field. Here turn right through the gate and walk down the next field to the stile which you will see in the bottom left corner. There are more good views across to Cadbury Castle from here – look out for the dragon (see tinted box feature, page 58).

After the stile turn left along the lane heading away from Kitlake Farm. Follow this for just over half a mile. You start to climb

Walking across Raddon Hills

slightly and as the route flattens out again you will see the back of a corrugated barn on your left. As the lane bears right look out for a footpath sign pointing sharp left off the lane, back on yourself. Take this path, now passing the open front of the barn on your left, and continue ahead through the field with the hedge on your right. This is an elevated and airy stretch of walking with panoramic 360° views and windswept trees. It can be wonderfully wild up here in some weathers. Behind you to the right you can see Dartmoor.

Eventually you pass through another gate into the next field. Continue in the same direction to the gates ahead of you and through them into a third field. In this field continue ahead but now with the boundary on your left. Head towards the massive pine tree – you can't miss it. A long time ago there were more of these trees standing here: this survivor now stands as lone sentinel over Raddon Hills. A majestic sight. Hug it, if you are inclined, the tree deserves it.

From here head to the stile beyond the tree, cross it and bear diagonally right down the next field to a stile in the bottom boundary. This leads to the steps which you passed earlier. Go down them, turning right at the bottom to retrace your steps along the track past Raddon Hill Farm and Raddon Hill Lodge.

The Killerton Dragon

Legend has it that the Iron Age hillforts at Cadbury and Dolbury (part of the Killerton estate) each conceal hidden treasure. The Killerton Dragon guards both, flying nightly between the two, a distance of some six miles as dragons fly. In addition to his duties on the hillforts, the dragon is reputedly also the protector of the family at Fursdon House, not far from Cadbury. Occasionally one hears dissent about whether the dragon actually belongs to Killerton or Cadbury. The dragon knows for a fact that he isn't owned by anybody.

Beyond Raddon Lodge you have an option. When you reach the bend in their drive you can either go left to cross the stile and pick up the footpath which you came along earlier, retracing your steps along your outward route, or continue all the way down the increasingly stony drive beyond Raddon Lodge until you meet the lane. At the lane turn left, passing Raddon Court on your right which you may have noticed during the course of the walk from the elevated paths you have been on above it. Follow this lane all the way back to Thorverton and your car.

Lone pine on Raddon Hills

Walk 10
Tiverton

The Grand Western Canal, originally built to transport lime, has a far less industrial ambience nowadays. As a country park and nature reserve, it is a haven for birdlife and the towpath is popular with walkers who can follow it as far as Holcombe Rogus, 12 miles away. This short, circular route goes out along the towpath and returns along what was once a railway line. It is easy, level walking and takes in some idyllic areas of countryside close to Tiverton.

Map:	OS Explorer 114, Exeter & the Exe Valley 1:25 000
Start point:	Grand Western Canal Basin. Post code EX16 4HT. Grid ref SS962123
Directions to start:	Tiverton is easily found, north of Exeter on the A396 and is clearly signed off the A361 North Devon Link Road
Distance:	3½ miles / 5.6km
Parking:	There is a pay and display car park adjacent to the canal basin
Facilities:	Tiverton is a good-sized market town with all the facilities one would expect. Brown tourist signs direct you to the canal where you will find public toilets, a tea gardens and the Tiverton Canal Company (01884 253345) offering horse-drawn barge trips, rowing boats etc for those disinclined to do the walk
Nearby places to stay:	The Hartnoll Hotel (01884 252777); Bridge Guest House (01884 252804); Tiverton Hotel (01884 256120)
Possible birds include:	Coot, dunnock, green woodpecker, kingfisher, mallard, moorhen, mute swan, robin
Authors' tip:	Try and work in a visit to Tiverton Castle (01884 255200). This wonderfully historic private home is open to the public from Easter until the end of October on Thursday, Sunday and bank holiday afternoons

From the car park go up to the canal basin and turn left along the towpath. Follow this as it leaves Tiverton, passing between pretty gardens in which you will frequently see feeding stations for the myriad water birds who are welcomed by local residents. The towpath passes under the William Authers Footbridge and, a little further on, under Tidcombe Bridge. The houses of Tiverton begin to drop away and the canal is now travelling through farmland.

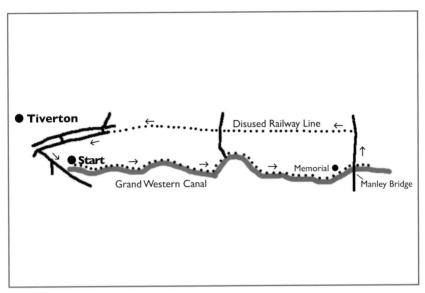

This is a beautiful stretch of water spanned in places by splendid oak trees. Pass under Warnicombe Bridge and just before the next bridge you will see a memorial to Roger Moore and Martin Archard, the crew of a Canberra Bomber which crashed here in 1961. Remnants of this crash were discovered in 2003 when the canal was dredged and polluted silt discovered along with bits of aircraft.

The next bridge is Manley, immediately after which you leave the towpath at a gate which leads into a little parking area. From here emerge onto the lane and turn right for about 100m. This is part of Sustrans Route 3 and the lane soon goes over a bridge at the far end of which you will see another Sustrans sign. Follow this off the lane as it directs you down a sloping path to a broad, tree-flanked track. This was once a branch line of the Great Western Railway (see tinted box feature, page 28) along which The Tivvy Bumper engine (now housed in Tiverton Museum) used to run. On a sunny day the dappled light down here is truly beautiful.

Beside the canal

Back towards Tiverton along the old railway

Walk ahead along the broad track as it heads back towards Tiverton. This is another lovely stretch of walking. The houses of Tiverton start to reappear and the path eventually emerges through a gate with a rather ornate signpost for the Sustrans National Cycle Network. Bear left across the grass and follow the road ahead, with houses on your left. This is Old Road.

Keep ahead, passing the unostentatious St. James' Church on your right. At a T-junction bear left as Old Road passes The Glades and then bends left up Canal Hill. The pavement here is on the right. About 200m up Canal Hill you will see the entrance to the canal car park on your left. Cross over with care and seek your car.

Grand Western Canal

Since 1971 the Grand Western Canal has been a Country Park and was designated as a local Nature Reserve in 2005, but its original purpose was very different. Constructed during the first half of the 19th C., it originally ran from Tiverton to Taunton, part of a plan for a much more extensive canal system, transporting such commodities as lime and stone. The ascendancy of the railways brought an end to all this. During its history the canal has also been used commercially for washing sheep and growing water lilies. Nowadays all that remains is the stretch of just over 11 miles between Tiverton and Lowdwells on the Devon–Somerset border. The Somerset stretch of the canal closed during the 1860s and is gradually disappearing, but the Devon section was saved from losing its identity by the formation of a preservation committee in 1962. Old lime kilns can still be seen near the basin in Tiverton and towards the other end of the canal near Waytown Tunnel.

Bickleigh & Cadeleigh

This is a lovely varied route although it can be muddy in patches. It takes you high above the Exe Valley with glorious views across rolling countryside. There are a few ups and downs as you would expect in this area but nothing too dreadful and you'll find plenty of gates at which to get your breath back and admire the scenery. During the early stages of the walk you pass a stretch of river which hosts a heronry, so you have a good chance of seeing these prehistoric-looking birds. There is also the possibility of seeing roe deer.

Map: OS Explorer 114, Exeter & the Exe Valley 1:25 000

Start point: Bickleigh Bridge. Post code EX16 8RW. Grid ref SS937076

Directions to start: Bickleigh nestles in the Exe Valley, on the A396 between Exeter and Tiverton

Distance: 7½ or 6¾ miles / 12 or 10.9 km

Parking: On-road in village centre. Alternatively, if you are planning to eat at The Fisherman's Cot and ring them in advance they are usually happy to permit parking in their car park

Facilities: The Fisherman's Cot (01884 855237) serves food all day and has the added advantage of fabulous riverside views of Bickleigh Bridge – one of several to have reputedly inspired Simon & Garfunkel's Bridge Over Troubled Water. There is also The Trout Inn (01884 855596) and the excellent Charlotte's Kitchen (01884 855700) at Yearlstone Vineyard. The Cadeleigh Arms (01884 855238), which also serves good food, is en route

Nearby places to stay: The Fisherman's Cot (01884 855237); The Trout Inn (01884 855596)

Possible birds include: Blackbird, blue tit, buzzard, carrion crow, chaffinch, cormorant, dunnock, fieldfare, green woodpecker, heron, house sparrow, lapwing, magpie, pheasant, robin, snipe, starling, wren

Authors' tip: Although not en route Yearlstone Vineyard, just off the A396 north of Bickleigh, is well-worth visiting. Allow time to do this – see page 70

From Bickleigh Bridge take the road signposted to Crediton, passing The Fisherman's Cot on your left. The road soon goes over a small humpback bridge after which go right towards Cadeleigh. Keep on the lane past the redbrick house of Riverside

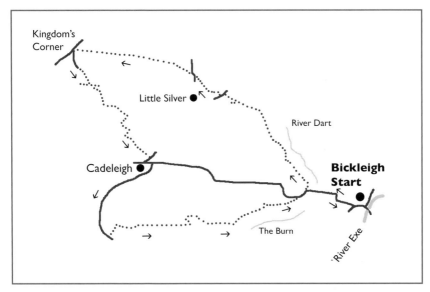

on your right. Just beyond their garages ignore the footpath right and continue on the lane. You reach a stone and white thatched house and after about 100m look out for the footpath sign on your right directing you off the lane through a farm gate. Beyond the gate walk along the top of the field with the hedge on your left.

As you reach the end of the field the River Dart (a different one to its much bigger brother in The South Hams) comes in to meet you on your right. Watch out for herons as you're now approaching the stretch of river which is their haunt. Keep ahead on this path through small fields with the hedge on your left and river on your right until just before you can go no further, at which point you meet a gate on your left. Leave the field through this gate and go right along the bridleway – a blue arrow directs you.

Once on the bridleway pass through a gate and continue with the track as it leads you past Dart Cottages. The River Dart has meandered away to the right and you will eventually see trout

Hair-raising task of getting the route right

ponds, another focal point for herons. Keep ahead on the track and as it levels out, after an ascending stretch, glance back across The Exe Valley in a south easterly direction towards the mast on Christ Cross (which you pass on the Silverton walk). The view is excellent.

The bridleway takes you through another gate and starts to descend – through the trees you may make out the buildings of Ashilford and Upper Dart ahead to the right of the track. As you reach the buildings glance up on your left to spot a tree house high above you. Just past these houses ignore the left hand footpath and keep ahead on the bridleway until you meet a lane.

Turn left on the lane for about 20m then turn right, as a bridleway sign directs you, along the drive to a cottage. Pass in front of the cottage on your right, please respect their privacy, and bear left over the little bridge. A few metres ahead you will see a gate with a blue arrow. Pass through here to walk between a stone shed on your left and a stone, block and cob barn on your right, passing through a second gate – arrows direct you clearly. Beyond the buildings continue on the track, uphill.

After ascending, the track levels out to pass between a lovely avenue of trees on a narrower path. Keep with it, noticing the hamlet of Little Silver with its converted chapel – the gravestones still standing – below to your left. The bridleway goes through

Along the path to Kingdom's Corner

another gate and narrows some more, then eventually emerges onto a lane. Turn right here and after 50m go left, on the signed bridleway. This is also the drive to Langley Farm.

As the drive to the farm bends left keep ahead on the track – you will see a blue arrow directing you. More glorious views as you puff uphill here. The path reaches an area where three field gates lead off. Look left here across to the Iron Age hillfort of Cadbury Castle which you will also see on the Thorverton walk. Look out for the dragon. From the wide area continue ahead on the narrow path which eventually emerges onto the lane at Kingdom's Corner.

Turn left and after about 10m left again. This is the drive to Well Bargains, Deep Ash, Willis Farm and Weston House. You will see a public footpath sign pointing along here. After Well Bargains and Willis Farms you will reach Deep Ash and here look out for the yellow arrow on the left, passing through the gate to then turn right and walk behind the red brick shed and garden boundary. Beyond the garden fence bear diagonally right across the field, arrows will help direct you. This line brings you to a field gate in the boundary with an adjacent stile.

Beyond the stile walk straight across the concrete drive to East Ridge Farm and into the grassy field ahead. Bear diagonally left across the field (another yellow arrow directs) and this will lead you to a gap in the boundary where an arrow points you straight down the next field with the boundary on your right. At the bottom turn right and then immediately left again, a kind of hedged chicane, to continue diagonally left downhill through the next field. This will lead you to a stile, cross this, followed by a stream, beyond which walk up the bank to meet a woodland path. Turn left on this lovely path, conifer woodland stretches uphill to the right and deciduous woodland down to the left in the valley. After a few hundred metres another arrow directs you sharp right up a broad track through the conifers. Take this and just before the top yet another arrow directs you left through the trees. Take this, occasional arrows on trees reassure you, and eventually you emerge from the conifers where another yellow arrow directs you ahead on a path through deciduous trees. The view opens up to your right.

This path leads to a stile on the right. Cross here and continue down the next field with the boundary on your left. In the bottom corner you will find a stream and an arrowed gate. Go through the gate and cross the stile immediately opposite, followed by a second stile. After the second stile bear left through the field towards a gate – the gate you need is the second on the left with a yellow arrow. Beyond this walk ahead into the field and then bear left to follow its boundary on your left. This leads to a gate in a fence with a footpath arrow pointing you to bear slightly right through the next field to meet a track, along which you turn left downhill. Keep ahead on this track for a very short distance and as it bends left you will notice a wooden gate ahead of you with another yellow arrow. Go through here and head downhill to a stile, beyond which you meet a metalled drive (note pond ahead).

Turn right along the drive away from the house. After approx 30m you will see another arrow directing you right across a field. Follow the path through the field in the direction of the arrow. There is a hill sloping steeply up to the left with the ground dropping away to your right. Keep on the grassy path climbing steadily uphill and keep with it as it curves left. As it continues to ascend you meet a field boundary on your right. Follow this uphill to meet a stile in the top corner.

Cross the stile and continue with the boundary on your right. When you reach the top right hand corner you will see another yellow arrow, continue ahead with the hedge on your right and keep in this direction through fields until you eventually reach farm buildings. Keep ahead here passing stables on your left and a red brick farmhouse, Glebelands, to continue along the drive beyond the buildings, emerging onto the lane at Cadeleigh Village Hall.

Turn right along the lane and at the T-junction turn left. Here the shorter option can be taken if you so desire. Those not wishing to partake of the rather good views along the Cadeleigh Court stretch of the walk can continue straight down the lane from Cadeleigh to Bickleigh, 1½ miles away, (there are pretty good views from here too), or straight into the embrace of The Cadeleigh Arms, as the mood takes you. Those on the longer route should take the next right, opposite The Cadeleigh Arms. Follow the lane passing St. Bartholomew's Church on your right. It's worth popping in here to admire the fabulous Leach Monument sculpted in Beer stone and marble.

Keep on this lane until, ½ mile beyond the church, you see a footpath on the right. Ignore this and ¼ mile further on take the footpath left off the lane. You are now on the concrete drive to Cadeleigh Court. Follow this as it winds past barns on the left. Stay on the main drive until, after almost ¾ mile, you see the elevated house of Cadeleigh Court ahead. As you reach the ivy-clad wall of the garden turn left. You will see a sign here for The Manor House as the path now continues to the drive for that property. Keep with the path as it passes the back entrance to Cadeleigh Court followed by the entrance drive to The Manor House, both right off the path. Just after The Manor House follow the yellow arrow round a right bend in the track, to walk through a fenced orchard.

Beyond the orchard pass through a gate and bear right down the track through the field to another gate. You will see a yellow arrow on this gate, pass through and continue on the broad, hedged track. Notice the clear meanders of the The Burn down to your right.

The path emerges below the house of East Court and, at the time of writing, passes a barn in the process of renovation. Pass round

Yearlstone Vineyard
The oldest Vineyard in Devon, Yearlstone enjoys a wonderful south-facing position above the Exe Valley and shares almost exactly the same latitude as the Moselle Valley. Established in 1976, the current owners, Roger and Juliet White, bought Yearlstone in 1994. As well as the 7½ acres of vines they have orchards, a winery and a fabulous café run by Charlotte Lampard. They also run wine courses and give vineyard tours. Juliette is a multiple-award-winning wine maker. Simone's favourite is Yearlstone No. 3 – a lovely rosé, which was silver medallist in the 2010 English & Welsh Wine of the Year Competition. James is rather fond of their red – No. 4.

the left hand end of the barn and continue past various buildings. The footpath is clearly signed through all this. Keep on the drive beyond the buildings as it winds past various houses, with lovely views to the right, and eventually reaches the lane. Turn right and you are on the home straight for Bickleigh.

Bickleigh Bridge

Stoodleigh

This is a beautiful route through wonderful countryside, but to achieve the views there have to be some steepish ascents and descents. Stretches of the walk can be extremely wet underfoot so wellies are strongly advised. The route takes you through some delightful, wildlife-rich woodland and you have a good chance of seeing deer.

Map: OS Explorer 114, Exeter & the Exe Valley 1:25 000

Start point: St Margaret's Church, Stoodleigh. Post code EX16 9PJ. Grid ref SS923188

Directions to start: Stoodleigh is clearly signposted off the A396 heading towards Bampton from Tiverton

Distance: 5½ miles / 8.9km

Parking: On-road near village centre

Facilities: There are no public houses or toilets in Stoodleigh, but don't let this put you off doing the walk. Nearby Bampton and Tiverton have plenty of facilities and The Exeter Inn (01398 331345) is the nearest hostelry, 1½ miles towards Bampton on the A396 from the point at which you turn off for Stoodleigh

Nearby places to stay: The Exeter Inn, Bampton (01398 331345); Quoit-at-Cross Farm, Stoodleigh (01398 351280)

Possible birds include: Blue tit, buzzard, carrion crow, fieldfare, great tit, pheasant, pied flycatcher, robin, rook, woodpigeon, wood warbler, wren

Authors' tip: Take a picnic as there's nowhere to eat around the village. Not far from the church you will find a little stall selling local produce which is usually worth a browse

From the church, with the porch behind you, walk along the path flanked by topiaried yews. Don't take the small path to the right but continue to the main gate. Cross the lane and continue through another gate along the hedged footpath opposite. You'll soon pass the pitch of Stoodleigh Cricket Club on your left.

Reach the lane and turn left for about 200m. At Kissing Gate Cross head over towards some stables and prior to their entrance gate you'll see a stile on the right. Cross this and head through the field

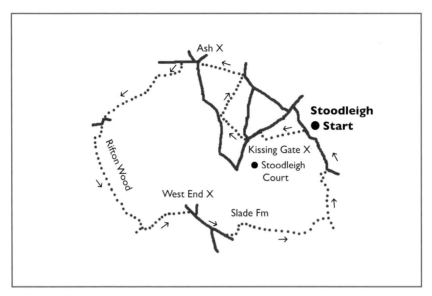

for 75m until a yellow arrow guides you through the hedge. Beyond this continue in the same line but now with the hedge on your right. In the corner of this field leave over a stile and turn immediately right along a track. Just before this track meets the lane you will see a footpath sign directing you left along another track. Take this. You are now walking along the edge of Ash Hill Plantation with the hedged boundary on your right. Keep on this path at the edge of the woodland until you meet a metal farm gate with a yellow arrow. Pass through here and continue ahead along the same line through a field. The trees of Marshlade Plantation are to your right beyond the fence and there are expansive views ahead of you towards Stoodleigh Beacon.

As the trees to your right end, continue ahead through the field to the gate at the bottom. Pass through here and go straight across the junction at Ash Cross, following the lane towards Aldridge Mill and Spurway Mill for 150m until you reach a bridleway on the left. This is also the drive to Wheatland Farm. Go down here until you see a house on the right after about 200m. Just beyond

In Rifton Wood

here look out for the bridleway sign on the left – this is an official reroute from what is shown on the OS map, to avoid Wheatland Farm buildings. Go through here and follow the direction of the blue bridleway arrow as it points you straight down the field with the hedge over to your left.

At the bottom cross the stream on the small bridge and follow the direction of the blue arrow to bear right beyond the bridge on the track. The stream is now down to your right and hedgerow to your left. Wheatland Farm is up to your right. At the end of this small field pass through a gap – still directed by arrows – and continue with the hedge to your left and the slope down to your right. In the next field you are directed diagonally right through the field on a clear path which begins to slope steeply down.

At the bottom go through a gate, cross the stream on a bridge and bear left. Follow this delightful, well-signed path through a few bridleway gates. There is an ancient, treed boundary to your right and the stream is down to your left. Soon the arrows direct you diagonally left to head down to the babbling stream. This is a lovely stretch of walking, follow the clear path until it eventually leads you to wade across the stream and pass through a gate onto the lane.

On the lane turn right, follow it as it bends left and you will see a wooden garage on the left and a bridleway sign. Leave the lane and follow the narrow bridleway which can be very muddy but is firmish at the edge! The path emerges in front of Rifton Lodge. Cross the stream and pass the lodge on your right – as always respect the privacy of the occupants. Beyond here you will see a post with a blue arrow directing you right up through the trees to a bridleway gate about 50m above and behind the Lodge.

Go through the gate and walk straight up through the trees of Rifton Wood in the direction of the arrow on the gate. About 150m from the gate you will see another reassuring blue arrow on a tree trunk, just to confirm that you are on the right path.

Keep ahead up through the trees, ignoring any deviating paths to left or right. It can be heavy going underfoot here. Eventually the path levels out. Beyond the boundary to your right you can see an open field. There is still woodland sloping down to your left. Stick

Towards Stoodleigh Beacon

with the bridleway as it winds along and about ¾ mile from Rifton Lodge, you reach the end of the woodland with a field ahead of you as well as to the right.

Here you will see a post with blue arrows indicating that the bridleway goes right. At this point you leave the bridleway and continue ahead through the trees, keeping the open field across the boundary to your right. About 50m from the post you will see a metal gate on the right. Turn left here and head steeply down through the trees to a wooden footbridge (sporting a reassuring yellow arrow) across a stream. This is about 300m down from the metal gate.

Beyond the footbridge continue up the field ahead, a good, steep, lung-clearer this. As you plod up this hill notice the ancient boundary also wending its way up the hill away to your left. Towards the top of the hill head towards the top right hand corner

The climb up out of Rifton Wood (don't let this put you off!)

and just below the corner you will find an arrowed gate. Pass through here and bear left across the field to the left hand end of the copse which you can see ahead.

In front of the copse you will find a stile. Cross it and turn right along the lane until you reach West End Cross. Keep ahead towards Washfield and Tiverton as far as Washfield Post Cross. Go left here and soon after take the public footpath left leading to Slade Farm. Pass the farmhouse on your left and turn immediately left to walk between the end of the house and barns. Yellow arrows guide you beyond the house to walk ahead on a track with a hedge on your left and further barns to your right.

At the end of these barns you will see another yellow arrow pointing you across to a farm gate. Beyond this continue through the field with the boundary to your left. Walk through a second field in the same line and as the hedge ends keep in the same direction and a fence comes in to meet you on the left. Glance left here to see the tower of Stoodleigh church peeping over the hilltop. (If this field is planted with crops keep to the edge rather than stomping through the middle.) A yellow arrow on the left fence directs you to continue down to the bottom of the field.

Stoodleigh Court

Occupying the site of the original Stoodleigh Manor, the present 19thC building was built for the Carew family. In the first quarter of the 20thC the estate was sold and the house was bought by Ravenswood School which relocated here from Paignton. The school closed in 1992 and the present owners have restored the building which is now used as a venue for corporate events and weddings. The picturesque lane leading to Stoodleigh from the A396 is still known as 'The Drive' and was originally the impressive private drive to Stoodleigh Court.

At the bottom, cross the stream on a plank bridge and swiftly after this a double stile. Beyond here walk through the bottom of the next field, stream to your left, and about 150m from the stiles bear left to cross the stream and go through a bridleway gate. After this head uphill to another gate and beyond this continue up in the same line with a fence on your right, to find yet another gate at the top of the hill. Go through here and bear left as directed down the field towards the stream. Cross the stile next to the gate, followed by a couple of small streams and bear right, as the arrow directs, on the path through trees. This is a rough, increasingly steep, uphill path. Pause to enjoy the views and when you reach the lane turn left. Keep on this back to the church, about 0.3 mile away.

Kennerleigh and Woolfardisworthy

Although there are a few slopes on this walk they are brief and not too challenging, and in no way detract from this short, gem of a walk. This route is a must, particularly if you don't have time for an all-day walk. There can be muddy patches and wellies are advised.

Map: OS Explorer 114, Exeter & the Exe Valley 1:25 000	
Start point: Kennerleigh Post Office and Stores. Post code EX17 4RS. Grid ref SS819073	
Directions to start: This tiny village is well off the beaten track, north of Crediton between Sandford and Black Dog	
Distance: 3½ miles / 5.6km	
Parking: On-road near village centre	
Facilities: There are no public toilets in Kennerleigh but it does boast a delightful post office and stores where sustenance for your walk can be purchased. A nearby pub is The Lamb Inn, Sandford (01363 773676)	
Nearby places to stay: Ashridge Farm, Sandford (01363 774292) is 1½ miles from Kennerleigh; The Lamb Inn, Sandford (01363 773676)	
Possible birds include: Blackbird, blue tit, buzzard, carrion crow, chaffinch, fieldfare, great tit, green woodpecker, linnet, little egret, magpie, robin, song thrush, starling, woodpigeon, wren	
Authors' tip: This tiny village hosts a really good website which is worth having a look at before you visit: www.kennerleighanddistrict.btck.co.uk	

Leave the stores with sufficient chocolate to keep you going and turn right out of the door. Pass the phone box, Garden Cottage and the entrance to the churchyard, all on your right. On the left of the lane look out for the public footpath sign which directs you along a track. Take this, passing a bungalow called Marchants on your left. Follow this level track for about 0.3 mile until it eventually leads you to some barns.

Pass through the gate in front of them and bear left – you will see a yellow arrow on the left hand end of the barn pointing you through the second of two gates on the left. Follow its direction

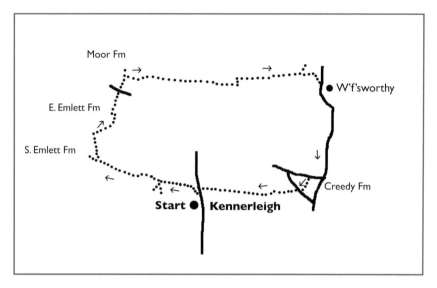

into the field which is ahead and to the left. Walk through the field, hedge on your left, you can see the buildings of South Emlett Farm ahead.

At the end of the field continue into the next field bearing slightly right as indicated and this leads you to another gate. Pass through and continue ahead with the hedge on your right, enjoying the views. About 150m from the gate you will find another gate on your right. Pass through here and walk across the track to go through yet another gate beyond. An arrow here points you diagonally left towards the left hand boundary and a gap, about 100m away, through which you enter the trees.

Head down into woodland and then follow the clear track. This feels like a very ancient route. The path bends about and can be quite muddy. Eventually you reach a crossing stream beside which is a beautifully mossy and fern-fringed fallen tree, which still has its roots in the ground and from whose trunk multiple smaller trunks have sprung vertically up to the light. It's worth doing the walk just for this tree. It looks like it's been there for ever.

Fern-fringed fallen tree

Cross the stream and go through the gate, then follow the track ahead. This winds up out of the trees to a tarmac drive. Cross the drive diagonally left to take the signed footpath about 20m away. Go along this path for about 15m then turn sharp right to a gate into a field, after which you turn left to follow the boundary on your left. There are easily-missable arrows to help direct you through this swerving bit – keep an eye open for them.

Follow the left hand boundary up the field to a gate. Go through, cross the lane, and take the footpath opposite to walk down the next field with the hedge now on your right. About 200m down this hedge you will find a stile. Cross this, followed by a plank bridge, then turn right along the hedge. Moor Farm is away to your left as you follow this hedge, bearing left just before the end of the field to another plank bridge and stile in the boundary, followed by another plank.

Frosty fields near Langham

Beyond this keep ahead through the field with a stream on your right. At the far side of the field you will find a high, stepped stile. Cross here and continue beyond it in the same line with a hedge on your left and Swanny Copse to your right. You will also see ponds down to your right although at the time of writing some young trees had recently been planted and they will probably obscure the further ponds as they mature.

The path eventually bends left to approach a house, keep on the track as it then veers right below the house, following the line of the fence with another two ponds to your right. Keep on the track to walk away from the house along their drive. Follow the drive for about 250m as far as the second eucalyptus tree, after which you will see a yellow arrow directing you left into a field. Follow this, keeping the hedge on your right, for 150m to another stile. Cross here and walk straight across the field to another stile in the far boundary. There are fabulous, rolling views down to your right from here. Cross the next stile, notice 1999 engraved on it, and walk through the field with the hedge on your left. You may be able to make out the tower of Woolfardisworthy church ahead of you. At the end of the field leave through the second gate on the left which has an arrow and turn right across the field in the same line as before towards the church and a gate into the churchyard. Take time to explore here.

Leave the church by the main gate and go down the path past some attractive cottages until you reach the lane, along which you turn right. Stay on the lane as far as Creedy Farm and Creedy Barn. Bear right with the lane, ignoring the option ahead, and pass the house of Creedy View on your left. You are climbing now and about 100m up the hill go left through a gate on the signed footpath. Turn right to follow the hedge on your right to the end of the field where you find a stile. Cross here and turn right on the lane for about 15m to another stile which has a very inventive dog flap. Pandora managed to work it out. Go left over this, or through the flap, and into the field to walk ahead with the hedge on your left. Soon you will see an arrowed gap in the hedge, pass through and continue in the same direction as before, now with the hedge on your right. Kennerleigh is in view ahead. At the next gate continue through the field beyond in the same line and when you enter a third field keep on, you will see barns ahead and to the left as you approach and a scattered assortment of farm machinery. Bear left beyond the barns to leave the field through a gate onto the lane opposite the church. Turn left here and you are back at Kennerleigh Post Office.

Woolfardisworthy

For such a curious village name it's all the more surprising that there are actually two of them in the same county. The second larger village of the same name is located some 40 miles away near Bideford in North Devon. Both are pronounced "Woolsery" locally. Woolfardisworthy is thought to derive from 'Wulfheard's homestead' – Oxford Dictionary of English Place Names (Eilert Ekwall, 4th ed., 1960). Whether both villages were named after the mysterious Wulfheard remains uncertain. This Woolfardisworthy is also referred to as Woolfardisworthy East to distinguish it from the other one in N. Devon.

Church of The Holy Trinity, Woolfardisworthy East

Walk 14

Withleigh

Wellies are advisable for this lovely walk through woodland and beside streams, just outside the village of Withleigh. It's an area that one of the authors has known since childhood and is a short and quite delightful route. There is a steep hill at the start and finish. Thongsleigh Wood was given to The National Trust by Mr Matteson in memory of his wife, Vera, and at his request it is called Buzzards after the birds they enjoyed seeing here. Since this first donation further areas of woodland have been added.

Map: OS Explorer 114, Exeter & the Exe Valley 1:25 000

Start point: National Trust Car Park – no post code. Grid ref SS905120

Directions to start: Withleigh is west of Tiverton on the B3137 towards Witheridge. In Withleigh you see the sign for the parish church bearing right. Turn left here off the B3137 (marked as 'no through road'). You are now on a narrow lane. Pass a couple of houses on your left and then, where a sign says 'unsuitable for motors', bear left with the lane (the track goes on ahead downhill) and immediately right into a small car parking area. Leave the car here

Distance: 2½ miles / 4km

Parking: In the designated parking area as described in directions to start

Facilities: None en route but The Mount Pleasant Inn, Nomansland (01884 860271) is less than 5 miles away; The Rose and Crown, Calverleigh (01884 246301) is under 4 miles away

Nearby places to stay: Great Bradley Farm, Withleigh (01884 256946)

Possible birds include: Blue tit, buzzard, carrion crow , dipper, dunnock, great spotted woodpecker, great tit, grey wagtail, kingfisher, robin, rook, wren

Authors' tip: For the gardeners, Withleigh Nursery is worth a visit and is clearly signed in the village

Leave the car park via the stile and descend the steep hillside to the gate in the bottom hedge. It is worth noticing the lovely rounded hillside ahead of you across the valley. Go through the gate and head left down the slope to where you see the track passing through the gap in the hedge. The River Dart is below you – the same River Dart which you will meet at Bickleigh. Turn left along this track into the field following the path with the hedge on your left.

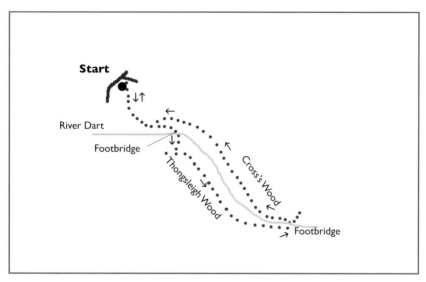

Continue through this field, ignoring any gates in the left hand hedge. At the end of the field cross the stile into the wood. This is Thongsleigh Wood and although not shown on the map as a public footpath it is marked as access land and belongs to The National Trust. Beyond the stile keep ahead to the footbridge a few metres away. Cross this and take the path which bears right through the trees. This soon meets a crossing track along which you turn left. Keep on this bridleway, as it passes through the trees with the river below to your left. This is a lovely moss- and lichen-rich woodland.

After about ¾ mile pass through a gate and continue along the track on the outskirts of the wood. The track emerges from the trees and becomes a grassy path. Follow this, until you see a footbridge a little further on, on your left. Head for this.

The walk continues over the footbridge but there is also a footpath to the right here along the banks of the river. This is an idyllic spot for an amble if you so wish, before continuing across the bridge and re-entering the woodland. Here you see another National

On the way back....

Trust sign which shows that you are now in Cross's Wood. Follow the path next to the river which is now on your left (there is also a footpath bearing right from the bridge which you ignore). As the river meanders away left keep ahead on the path. Pass through a gate and you will see the bridleway forking off to the right and the footpath continuing ahead. Keep on the footpath as it goes through a meadow. As the right hand hedge bends away up the slope keep straight on, the river rejoins you, to a stile. Cross the stile and re-enter the wood keeping on the path and ignoring tracks to right or left, unless you wish to explore. (You will eventually see the bridleway rejoining from your right before going off left again a little later.)

Buzzards (Buteo buteo)

One of the most frequently seen birds of prey in the UK, Culm Valley Publishing adopted this bird as its logo since buzzards are so often seen soaring over the woodland which flanks our valley. Their mewing call is a distinctive sound. Buzzards pair for life and breed throughout the country. They feed on carrion, small birds and mammals – and occasionally earthworms when provisions are short. Sometimes they are seen 'riding thermals' in groups of 20 or more. As a child, one of the authors nursed a poisoned buzzard back to health, after which it was successfully released back into the wild. Our cat was very good about providing dead mice and handling a bird like this was quite an experience. The one on our logo was quite obliging about being photographed and has the advantage of claiming no modelling fee.

Buzzards at Withleigh

Beside the River Dart

The path emerges from the wood at a wooden gate. Walk through the field in the same direction with the hedge and fence on your left until you reach its end. Go through the gate at the end of the field and now continue in the same direction with the hedge on your right. You reach the gap in the hedge which you passed through at the beginning of the walk – head right up the field to the gate above you. Go through and retrace your steps up the steep incline to where you car awaits.

Rackenford

Rackenford is set in a very elevated position and this lovely walk follows clear paths through varied terrain. Since the starting point at Rackenford is so high the walk itself is fairly level with no serious inclines. It can be very muddy in places and there is some lane walking.

Map: OS Explorer 114, Exeter & the Exe Valley 1:25 000

Start point: Village Centre. Post code EX16 8DT. Grid ref SS851183

Directions to start: Rackenford is clearly signposted off the A361 (North Devon Link Road) about 10 miles north west of Tiverton. Alternatively approach via the B3137 from Tiverton to Rackenford

Distance: 5¾ miles / 9¼ km

Parking: On-road in village

Facilities: The Stag Inn (01884 881369) is the oldest pub in Devon; there is also a very good community shop and post office (01884 881740)

Nearby places to stay: The Old Forge (01884 881588)

Possible birds include: Buzzard, carrion crow, chaffinch, coal tit, collared dove, fieldfare, great spotted woodpecker, great tit, house sparrow, lapwing, nuthatch, pheasant, raven, robin, rook, starling, wren

Authors' tip: Rackenford has a beer festival every two years and an annual 'village day'. Check their village website to confirm dates: www.rackenford-devon.co.uk

---

All Saints' Church is a solid, country church and the walk starts by leaving the churchyard via the lych-gate. Walk along the lane away from the church, passing the little thatched shelter for the restored Trinity Well on your left. The working pump in here enables walkers' boots to be cleaned when you return to this spot at the end of the walk.

About 20m from the church turn left along the lane in front of the tennis court and after another 200m go left again, passing The Old Rectory and Stables on your left and then the drive to Lanelands Farm on your right. 80m beyond here you reach a footpath on your right. Take this and walk through the field following the left hand

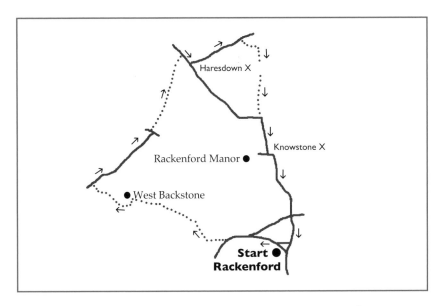

Haresdown X

Knowstone X

Rackenford Manor ●

● West Backstone

←
Start ●
Rackenford

boundary. The field narrows to reach a gate. Beyond here follow the direction of the yellow footpath arrow as it points you right onto a path flanked by tree-topped banks. This is a lovely part of the walk. Ignore any gates to left or right and keep on this path until it crosses a stream and emerges into a field across a stile.

Head diagonally right across this field as it slopes up to the opposite hedge, you will see a pond down to your left. In the top boundary find a gate with another yellow arrow. Pass through this gate and head diagonally left up to the corner of the next field. To your right you can see the buildings of Worthy Farm. Cross the stile in the corner of the field and now you see West Backstone ahead of you. Another arrow directs you to head down the sloping field in line with these farm buildings and as the right hand boundary comes to meet you, you will see a stile below you entering a copse.

Beyond the stile head down into the trees, crossing the stream on the wooden footbridge. Bear left up the opposite side of the copse

Fortuna

on the trodden path to a wooden gate about 30m from the bridge. Pass through here – there is a sign welcoming walkers to West Backstone. After the gate turn immediately right and follow the fence up to another gate through which you enter a little triangular field. In here continue up, with the boundary on your right, to another gate beyond which you join a track.

Before the next gate about 40m along the track, look out for the statue to the Goddess Fortuna who was placed here to give thanks for this farm's escape during the outbreak of foot and mouth in 2001. The Latin inscription by Fortuna's feet, *Stet Fortuna Domus*, translates as 'let the fortune of the house stand'. Interestingly, this is also one of the mottos of Harrow School. A little further on we find another inscription *Te pauper ambit sollicita prece ruris colonus*. This is from Horace and means 'the poor farmer addresses you with anxious prayer'.

Ponder the inscriptions, then pass through the gate to turn immediately left through another gate, passing the front of West Backstone farmhouse. Just past the house keep ahead on a track. A few metres further on there is a meeting of paths. Go right here, an arrow directs, and continue on the tree-lined track as it soon bears right again, ignoring any gates to left or right. About 40m after the second bend you meet two gates. Pass through the left of these, it has an arrow, into a field and after the gate walk diagonally right to the far corner of this field.

The Two Moors Way   *The leaning tree*

Here you find another yellow footpath arrow. Pass through the
wooden gate, immediately followed by a metal hurdle, and bear
right for a few metres through the field to a gate with another
yellow arrow. Go through this gate and then through the next
small field, passing between wooden sheds on your right and a
house, Creacombemoor Cottage, on your left. Leave the field
through more wooden gates and turn right along the drive, leaving
the house behind you.

At the end of the drive turn right along the lane. This is now part
of the Two Moors Way, a long distance footpath between Exmoor
and Dartmoor. On a clear day there are good views from this lane.
In about ½ mile you reach a T-junction with Rose Ash and South
Molton off to your left, Rackenford and Tiverton to the right.

Cross the road and bear slightly left to join a clear bridleway. This
is still the Two Moors Way. Walk straight ahead along the track

with ancient, tree-topped banks on either side of you. This is another particularly lovely stretch of the walk with some wonderful trees and moss-softened banks. Ignore any gates to left or right and stick with the track – you will periodically pass bridleway / Two Moors Way signs to reassure you. Eventually you will cross a high, stepped wooden stile and after another 200m or so the track veers right to emerge from the trees almost a mile after you left the lane and first entered them. Now bear left to follow the obvious waymarkers as they lead you, with the boundary on your left, across a couple of hundred metres of scrubland to a lane. Turn right here, leaving the Two Moors Way. You can hear traffic from the North Devon Link Road in the distance.

Within ¼ of a mile, at Haresdown Cross, turn left along the lane signposted to East Anstey and after another ½ mile turn right at the bridleway sign. Pass through the gate and head across the field towards a stand of tall trees, one of which leans very firmly against its neighbour. It's been like this for a long time. Pass through these trees and you will see a gate beyond sporting a blue bridleway arrow. Go through here and follow the track past the trees of Great Plantation on your left. Keep on in this direction, eventually leaving the plantation behind you as you go through another gate and continue in virtually a straight line with a fence on your left.

Eventually you pass through a wooden gate under an old oak tree to emerge onto the lane. Take a moment to look up into this tree which is festooned with trailing clumps of lichen – a sign of very clean air. It's probably easier to see this in the leafless time of winter. Join the lane and walk straight ahead in the same direction as before. You are now walking through a lovely wood, full of moss-covered gnarly bits. The trees on the right are part of the estate of Rackenford Manor.

This lane emerges at Knowstone Cross. Turn left here and follow the lane, watching out for traffic, back to Rackenford village, clearly signposted all the way.

Trinity Well

Devon is dotted with Holy Wells and Rackenford's natural water supply, housed in a delightful cob and thatch pump house, was originally one of these. For centuries it was the primary water supply for the village, its pure spring water reputedly being good for eyesight (cf. Heal-eye Stream near Silverton). In the 1950s mains water arrived in the village so the well became obsolete and was capped. After years of discussion and fundraising by the parish council the supply was restored in 2009  and a working pump now invites walkers to clean their boots. Make use of it – it is redolent of an age when the acquisition and transport of water for day-to-day tasks was a strenuous undertaking and when water was a more highly-regarded commodity.

View from the Two Moors Way

Other books published by Culm Valley Publishing

Title: *A Dozen Dramatic Walks in Devon*
Authors: James Clancy and Simone Stanbrook-Byrne

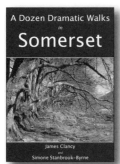

Encompassing the best of Devon, this book takes the walker to glorious coastline, expansive moorland and deep gorges, as well as picturesque river valleys and idyllic villages. More than just a walking guide, each route includes details of refreshment stops, places to stay and places of interest. Historic notes, authors' tips and natural history pointers are included. It will appeal to photographers who will find plenty of subject matter on these fabulous routes.
Walks: Drewsteignton & the Teign Gorge; Noss Mayo; Little Switzerland; Meldon & the High Tors; Trentishoe & the Heddon Valley; North Devon's Glorious Beaches; East Portlemouth; The Doone Valley; Bolt Head & Soar Mill Cove; Bigbury-on-Sea; Tavy Cleave; Branscombe & the Hooken Undercliff

Publication date: January 2011
Format: Paperback   **Pages**: 88pp
ISBN: 978-1-907942-00-6   **Price**: £5.99

Title: *A Dozen Dramatic Walks in Somerset*
Authors: James Clancy and Simone Stanbrook-Byrne

These twelve circular routes, which incorporate some of the county's most stunning scenery, are for walkers who like drama, amazing views and a sense of accomplishment at the end of the day. Taking in some of Somerset's most beautiful landscapes, this book is primarily aimed at those who don't mind putting a little effort into their day's walking. However, options on shorter or easier routes are given where practical for those who prefer less of a challenge.
Walks include: Cheddar Gorge; Exmoor Coast; Dunkery Beacon; Simonsbath; Quantocks; Mendips; etc.

Publication date: Spring 2011
Pages: 88pp
ISBN: 978-1-907942-02-0
Format: Paperback
Price: £5.99

Title: *A Dozen Dramatic Walks in Cornwall*
Authors: James Clancy and Simone Stanbrook-Byrne

The drama and beauty encountered in Devon and Somerset is now continued further west in Cornwall with no lessening of the quality of walking.
In keeping with other titles in the series, each route includes details of local watering holes for refreshment, places to stay and nearby places of interest. Historic notes, authors' tips and pointers on natural history are also included.
Walks include: Bodmin Moor; Tintagel; Lamorna Cove; Helford Estuary; Talland Bay/Polperro; etc.

Publication date: September 2011
Pages: 88pp
ISBN: 978-1-907942-03-7
Format: Paperback
Price: £5.99

Orders can be placed at www.culmvalleypublishing.co.uk
or alternatively by telephone on 01884 849085